T0077796

On the Cutting Edge:
Redemption

By J.J. Luepke
© 2010

Order this book online at www.trafford.com
or email orders@trafford.com

Most Trafford titles are also available at major online book retailers.

Printed in the United States of America.

ISBN: 978-1-4269-3787-3 (sc)
ISBN: 978-1-4269-3788-0 (e)

Trafford rev. 12/28/2010

www.trafford.com

North America & international
toll-free: 1 888 232 4444 (USA & Canada)
phone: 250 383 6864 ♦ fax: 812 355 4082

I dedicate this book to the Lakeview Writer's Club and its facilitator, S.A.M., who have been instrumental in honing my writing skills.

Chapter One
Trouble Brewing

Cassandra Coven set down the dumbbells with a thud. She sprang onto the queen-sized bed, emerald green satin teddy ruffles floating on the breeze. Straddling the equally-fit but white-haired man lounging there, she pinned him with her icy green stare.

"I just don't know what to do with her," she pouted. "Her work is good, but lately she's been hounding me for more recognition."

"Josie Buchannon is a talented young woman," Cass's lover replied. "She has earned her share of rewards. After all, how many new clients has she brought in during the nine months she's been with Sanderson & Sons Advertising Agency? More than you have during the past four years."

"Aw, Lew. That's not fair!" Cass shrieked as he tickled her. She swept his face with her shoulder-length burnished blonde hair and pulled away. "It's not fair at all because she grew up here and knows everyone! They probably felt sorry for her and wanted to give her a hand at her first real job out of college. The proof will be in the repeat business."

Cass slid off the bed and into a matching satin mini robe. Tying it about her, she glided over to the dresser and retrieved her cigarettes. Lighting one up, she returned to the foot end of the bed and glared at Lew Sanderson for an answer.

"Well, darling, we are a small firm, but we could make up a title to appease her," Sanderson drawled. "'Creative Director' might work. And, a tiny raise to show how much she means to us …"

"Tiny is right," Cass said, then snorted. "I could replace her in a heartbeat!"

"Now, now!" Sanderson chided. "Your green streak is showing."

"Sor-ry! Cass said sarcastically. "She didn't have to learn everything the hard way, like I did. She didn't have to go to work right out of high school to support her family."

"Well, she didn't have much of a family to support," Sanderson came to Josie's defense. "Remember, she's got only her dear old grandmother who probably lives on Social Security. Give the kid a break. I can afford it. Besides, I think she's earned it; and, who's the boss?"

"You are, Lew," Cass resigned with a sigh. "As long as I come in second, right behind you!" Then she stumped out her cigarette and rejoined him in bed. It was the weekend; and, she didn't want to deal with office politics anymore until Monday.

Monday morning, the weather was as dreary as the atmosphere inside the office of Sanderson & Sons Advertising Agency. Everyone had reported to work on time; but, the mid-winter doldrums had set in.

The intercom beeped, startling Josie out of her daze. She had been thinking about the dull weekend she had just spent cleaning house for her grandmother. Grams was normally a tidy person; but, she required assistance in returning all the holiday decorations to their usual year-round hiding places. It had been depressing work.

"Josie," Cass's voice came through the phone set. "Please come to my office."

"Be right there, Boss!" Josie replied, then grabbed a notebook and pen – just in case. Stepping down the hall took a mere ten seconds; but, Josie dreaded every step. Her mind flickered over the passed couple of weeks' work, searching for any reason whatsoever that Cass might have found to fire her. Josie was a little gun-shy after the way Sherry Ingram had been let go last summer.

It was shortly after Josie had been hired that Cass began complaining about Sherry's work. Josie was still trying to get a handle on her own duties to worry about Ingram's output; however, the more she paid attention, the more she was stupefied about the complaints. Ingram, a red-haired spit-fire, was an average worker and an enjoyable coworker. She worked hard to support two school-aged children. Ingram occasionally took an afternoon off to take a sick child to the doctor; but, nothing noteworthy. Yet, Cass found every excuse she could to publicly berate Ingram's work. Until finally, Ingram – having had enough – turned in her resignation. Josie would never forget that day. Coven called everyone to the foyer to say good-bye to Ingram. It was like one last slap in the face as the manager stood nearby Sherry's desk watching her pack up her belongings, and then march her to the door. That was the very same day Sherry had turned in her letter of resignation. Cass didn't trust Ingram enough to let her finish the two-week notice she had given. Since then, Josie had been on her toes to dot her I's and cross her T's. She didn't want to give Cass a reason to let her go, too.

Tapping on the door to the manager's office, Josie peered inside. Cass motioned for her to enter and be seated. Josie took an uneasy position on the edge of the flowered couch that rested along one wall. She smoothed her navy skirt and patted her notebook.

"I brought my notebook in case I need to take notes," Josie said, tentatively.

"You won't be needing that," Coven replied, crossing her tweed jacketed arms and leaning her elbows on the oak desk. "I've got good news for you."

"Oh?" Josie asked, dumbfounded.

"Based on the good work you've been doing, the company is naming you 'Creative Director'," Coven said with raised eyebrows. She got up from behind her desk and paced around to where Josie was seated. Extending her hand, she added, "We're giving you a $25 a week raise, to boot. Congratulations!"

Josie's mouth dropped open. Her eyes flitted between the proffered hand and Coven's face. She couldn't' believe her ears! Finally, she grasped the hand before it was withdrawn.

"You are management, now," Coven said, her sultry voice nearly purring. "We'll have to watch each other's backs from now on. If you hear the others talking about me, you'll have to tell me. If you find them goofing off, let me know. Okay?"

"You don't want me telling them to get to work, or anything?" Josie asked. "Do I have any authority with this title?"

"Let's see," Coven teased, tapping her forefinger to her temple. "You have the authority to ask Donna to type letters for you and place calls – that sort of thing. We'll share her as a secretary. Then, there's Jessica. You can rely more on her to do research for you. And, of course, you'll be working more closely with Hildy to produce you're animated work on computer. However, I wouldn't give any direct commands to her. You know how temperamental production people are. You'll have to handle her with kid gloves. Ask, not order. You know."

4

"Well, I wouldn't want her to take my head off, or anything," Josie admitted. For a cat-lover who enjoyed classical music, that was one heckuva temper Hilda Schumacher possessed. Maybe those were just tools Hildy needed to soothe the savage beast inside, Josie thought.

"Good, then that's settled," Coven continued. "Your promotion is effective immediately, and your raise will be reflected on your next pay check. By the way, what's on your schedule for this afternoon? We should go out to celebrate and to plan strategy.

"Sounds good to me. I've got calls to make until 12:30, but after that, I'm free," Josie replied.

"Okay. I will meet you at the door at 12:35, then," Coven said by way of dismissal. *Like Sungsu said, 'Keep your friends close, but your enemies even closer,'* Coven thought to herself as Josie left her office.

Chapter Two
Hope for the Best

The remainder of the morning went by in a blur for Josie. Her heart was light; and, her head was lighter still. The lift filtered through to every client she contacted and produced positive results. By the time 12:30 rolled around, Josie had set six more interviews with prospective clients. Still exuberant from the fruitful morning, Josie met Cass at the front door. Buttoning their long wool coats against the blustering northwest wind, they stepped out to the already-running Lexus Coven drove.

"This is a very luxurious car," Josie commented as she caressed the butter-soft leather seats. "It must be nice to have a company car – especially one with a sun roof."

"Yes, it is, except I can't use the sun roof on a day like today!" Coven replied. "Did you bring your notepad along? We will be going over your prospect list and jotting down ideas to work up."

This was the first time they would actually be comparing notes, as it were, Josie was aware. However, there were several times over the passed few months that the two of them seemed to be thinking along the same lines. Josie would come up with a hot new lead or develop a show-stopping ad for an existing client only to find Cass had come up with the very same one. If Josie was lucky enough to share her ideas first, Cass would end up sharing the credit. If Coven beat her to the punch line, Cass somehow came out with a solo by-line. Josie had chalked it up to bad timing and/or the fact that Cass was the manager of the agency.

"Great minds think alike," was the worn-out comeback Coven used when that happened. Josie began to wonder about the coincidence of how many times their minds had thought alike. She barely hung in with the conversation on the way to the Lake City Lounge & Supper Club where they would dine on the company expense account. Her mind was caught up in ways to test a theory that was forming concerning the originality of her boss' ideas. After all, Coven had access to all the E-mail that came into the agency, including those mailings Josie sent from home. She also had access to all the desks and work areas in the building. It also occurred to Josie that Cass was always the first to arrive and the last to leave every day. She said she liked to lock up and take responsibility for all the lights being shut off, and the like.

It was right down to business as soon as the two women were seated. Cass pulled a pocket-sized notebook and an elegant pen from her purse. Josie followed suit with her legal pad and dime store pen.

"So, how'd your phone session go this morning? Any new leads?" Cass asked nonchalantly.

"It was great! I set up appointments with six new clients and confirmed filming dates with three current advertisers," Josie gushed. "Having been promoted seems to have had a positive influence on my performance. Thank you very much!"

"You're welcome," Cass said. "Of course, now that you're management, you'll have to put in more time developing a longer lead list and coming up with fresh ideas. What's your game plan for that?"

Josie had been anticipating this line of questioning. Cass could be as direct and unrelenting as a district attorney embroiled in a hot court case. Unfortunately, the two miles to the eating establishment hadn't been long enough to form a complete strategy.

"Well, one thing I thought of – in this short time – was to have a new sign painted for the outside of our building," Josie scrambled. "If we want to be the advertising agency of the future, we have to show people how proud we are of our work. I think our current sign is outdated. It doesn't reflect our vision or our talents."

"Interesting," Cass said noncommittally, making a note on her pad. After a drag on yet another cigarette, she primed the pump. "What about new leads – actual names and phone numbers. We can't expect them to flood the office just because we put up a new sign."

"Okay, you're right. How about offering discounts or an additional week's advertising for a set number of referrals, say five or ten? Or for every referral that pans out. Along the lines of our own advertising, we should put Hildy on developing anew television ad for our agency reflecting that same vision I mentioned."

"Hmmm," Cass considered it. "That may take more time than we have in a paid work day. Why don't you see what you can come up with over the next couple of weekends and run it by me before we go to Hildy? She has her hands full as it is; however, if we went to her with a good idea or two, she could put some finishing touches on it."

Cass scratched some more illegible notes on her pad, then looked up at Josie. "The referral thing will take some time, too. Got any special leads up your sleeve?"

"I was saving this 'til last," Josie admitted, biting her bottom lip, "but I have friends who work at Agre's Auto Sales and Marshall's Food Market who think I have a shot at their accounts."

"They advertise with agencies in the Big Apple," Cass said. "What makes you think they would come back to Sanderson & Sons?"

"Yes, they went with Ed Braun and Ted Furley when they left," Josie said with a sigh. She realized that might be a sore subject since those gentlemen left because Coven was named agency manager in their place. "However, Braun and Furley have been hard to reach. And, they no longer represent home-town values or keeping business in-town. The clients are becoming increasingly dissatisfied with their service, in proportion with the ever-rising prices those big city firms are charging. I think we have an excellent chance at reclaiming them."

Truthfully, the idea had just popped into Josie's head. She was scraping for impressive ideas that sounded plausible. Yet, this could turn out to be a good test for Cass' true intentions. If she beat Josie to the punch at contacting them, she would know for sure just where she stood.

"Now that is a plan we can sink our teeth into," Cass said, nodding and writing. "Over that next couple of nights, why don't you come up with ideas to present to them when we contact them? You want to be prepared."

Just then their salads arrived and the conversation changed to food and fashions for the remainder of their stay. When they were finished, Cass drove Josie around town and stopped at a dress shop, presumably to discuss their advertising campaign. However, Coven spent a couple of C-notes on clothes and jewelry and didn't even get around to talking shop.

Back in the Lexus, Cass turned to Josie with a knowing grin.

"As management on a salary, we can take a few side trips as long as we get our work done," she said with a wink. "The office help wouldn't understand, so let this be our little secret. Besides, it's like greasing the elbow. The dress shop may increase their advertising if we patronize them."

Josie gave her a neutral grunt and sat back to reflect on all the work she would have to take home because of the time the two of them just wasted. The only compensation was that she was with her boss, so she shouldn't get into trouble over this excursion.

Back at the office, the telephone messages had piled up for both manager and creative director. Josie plucked her message slips from the bin on Donna Schmidd's desk and attempted a smile for the receptionist. The expression of thanks died on her lips as the mousy young woman drilled Josie with a brow-furrowed look of disdain and turned back to her computer screen.

I wonder if she suspects where we've been and what we've been doing, Josie thought. *Or rather, what we haven't been doing.* Once again, Josie was glad she had been with her supervisor and wouldn't get called on the carpet for playing hooky.

Josie returned to her desk and began furiously sketching ad ideas on the story boards stacked there. Using colored pencils and charcoal, she pulled together some ideas that had been floating around in the back of her mind all day. Staying busy was the only way to dispel the feeling of dread and doom that had haunted her since summer. It twisted her stomach into knots and sent bile floating in her throat. However, she didn't dare let it get the best of her. The middle of winter would be no time to be hunting for a new job.

Give your all, Grandma had always told her, *even if others get the credit.*

By the end of the week, Josie had her suspicions confirmed. While she had been busy developing campaign ideas for Agre's and Marshall's, Cass had gone ahead and set up interviews with them on her own. She did take Josie along to share her marketing ideas, good ones they liked, but again shared the credit for welcoming them back into the fold.

"They loved your ideas!" Cass exclaimed on their return to the office. "Using local kids to promote their products was a stroke of genius. I really respect your work, Josie."

"Is that why you keep taking credit for it?" Josie blurted. "You knew I was planning to call those companies myself because of my contacts there."

"Don't be such a spoil sport, Josie," Cass said threateningly. "That kind of attitude won't get you anywhere. We're a team here. If you don't like it, don't let the door hit you on the way out."

Stunned and properly rebuked, Josie slunk back to her desk. *What would Grandma say about this development?* Bite your tongue, for one, Josie thought. She took out a legal pad and started doodling. It was a habit she developed in high school and carried with her through college. Whenever she couldn't focus on the class work assigned, Josie would doodle. It allowed her to look busy, yet left her mind free to work through whatever was disturbing her at the time. This time it was a boss who stole her ideas and threatened to fire her if she didn't put up with it. Although Grandma was still with the living, Josie realized that not only was she, herself, an adult now, but this was not a safe problem to take to her beloved relative.

"Hope for the best and plan for the worst," was another of Grandma's favorite sayings. *Okay*, Josie thought, *how can I plan for the worst?*

Chapter Three
Plan for the Worst

That first weekend wasn't spent so much on developing agency ad ideas as sketching out a plan of defense. Josie sat at her home computer scheming up scenarios which might arise in the course of the remainder of her employment with Sanderson & Sons. If things went badly, she would have to have her resume handy at the very least. So, that was the first item on the agenda: update her resume and print it on ivory linen stationary. Once that was accomplished, she addressed envelopes from a list of agencies in New York City to whom she would send them.

In the meantime, she had to think of ways to avoid Coven and keep her from stealing any more of her ideas.

First, no more E-mails to work. I need to download them onto a disk and carry it on my person from now on, Josie thought. *Secondly, no more leaving work on my desk for anyone to see – especially her.* But that won't stop her from asking, and by every rule in the book, as manager, she has the right to see your work, came the unwelcome thought. *I guess I'll have to try to find ways to stay out of reach until staff meetings. That would be a neutral arena to unveil my ideas with witnesses as to their originality. If I'm her main source for her "great ideas", she won't have any back-up. What happens if she gets frustrated or angry with that set-up?*

That was the $64 million dollar question. The only answer that came to mind was that if something horrible happened, she would either be out on the street or be taking her case to Lewelyn Sanderson, the owner. Josie wasn't so certain the latter would prove fruitful. Office gossip had it that Cass slept her way into the manager's office and was still having an affair with the owner of the agency. Not to mention the fact that Mr. Sanderson seldom set foot in the office anymore, claiming to be semi-retired. He would be hard to reach in either case. That made the resume plan all the more alluring and vital.

Resolving to cover all the bases, Josie sent out the resumes. It was her Plan B; although, she hoped it wouldn't come to that. She loved working in her home town and being able to take care of her grandmother. Josie also loved living in the Victorian Drama style home provided by her parental substitute. Life couldn't get any better than this, from that standpoint. Time would tell if this ideal set-up would be allowed to continue.

Sunday evening was a flourish of sketching as Josie worked up story boards for each and every client with which she was schedule to meet this week. Her intensity brought raised eyebrows from Grandma Buchannon, but Grandma knew when not to ask questions. She knew it would not be prudent to interrupt Josie while she was in her creative mood. Artists are that way, she remembered. Josie took after her mother in that respect. If she had lived, Josie's mom would have been a successful painter.

At Monday morning's staff meeting, Josie was ready with her work. She even went in early to set up the poster boards on easels in the conference room. She proudly displayed the crafty ideas she had developed the night before. Hildy offered some useful technical suggestions. Jessica Springer volunteered to more deeply research the market on one weaker idea. It was in an area of great interest to her, Springer said. Jotting down Hildy's ideas and thanking Jessica, Josie braced herself for what could only be hair-raising remarks from her boss. Much to her surprise, Cass was quietly making notes of her own and nodding in contemplation.

"Good work, team," Coven commented. "I like to see us all working together. Josie, keep us posted on how the clients react to your ideas. I have financial meetings during most of those slots. Also, I will be out of the office most of Wednesday and Thursday visiting prospective clients and running errands. I trust you kiddies can get along without me for a few hours!"

Everyone laughed while Josie took note of how Cass was dressed. Her boss was wearing one of her sexy little numbers again. The copper mini dress had long chiffon sleeves and a neckline that was a little too revealing for the office. It looked great on Cass, but Josie couldn't help thinking it would make a better choice for an evening on the town than meetings with coworkers and clients. Josie shook her head. If it wasn't Saturday night dresses, it was bibbed overalls. Granted, Friday was casual day and the denim was allowed, but her boss lackFed a certain maturity in her wardrobe selections. It was just another reminder that Coven had no formal education. With that in mind, Josie sped back to her desk to prepare for her first client of the week.

The next two weeks sped by in much the same manner. Everything seemed to be flowing along as Josie had planned. She and Cass seldom crossed paths; and, when they did, it was usually at staff meetings. On the next two weekends, Josie poured over various angles to present on behalf of the agency. She was particularly relieved that the first Monday, when Cass apparently forgot Josie was working on the agency ads. It gave her a week's reprieve. This time, Grandma had asked her why she was bringing so much work home on the weekends. It just wasn't like her not to get it all done during the week.

"This is special, Grams," Josie had answered. "This project may reshape our whole business. This part is a new sign design to reflect our vision of the future. And, this – over here – is a television commercial I'm hoping will do the same thing. However, I'm not sure this segment here – is possible to create, even on computer. I'll have to ask Hildy."

Josie went into work early that Monday. She wanted to catch the production manager before the stocky German delved into her massive work load for the day. It started out as a simple request. Could this little idea work? Hildy got caught up in it and spent half an hour polishing off the entire presentation for Josie. By the time their boss called the staff meeting, Hildy had all but gift-wrapped the most important idea Josie had come up with in six weeks.

"I know I was supposed to run this by you first," Josie said by way of an apology, "but I had this little glitch I wanted to ask Hildy about. Before I knew it, she had the entire commercial set up on her computer. This disk contains that commercial you wanted for the agency. Do you want to see it now or save it for after the meeting?"

People like choices, Josie had heard somewhere along the way. She certainly hoped the two choices she presented would appease her boss right now. Having had the feeling Coven didn't like her authority or her orders questioned or disobeyed in any sense, didn't leave much room to hope these choices were satisfactory. A deadly hush blanketed the conference room as Coven took the disk from Josie. She stared at it momentarily then set it down on the table next to her notebook.

"I'll look at it later," Coven said darkly. "Be sure you stick around after the meeting so we can discuss it."

Without giving Josie another glance, Cass continued the staff meeting. There now was a trace of hardness to her facial expressions and her voice that seemed to age her 20 years. This was a hard-core, no-nonsense woman in action. Here was one who knew what she wanted and how to get it – the hard way. She could and would play hardball with anyone who crossed her. This fact was born out a couple of times when Coven dealt with the "Old Boys' Club" in town.

Last summer, they had sponsored an annual golf tournament that was frequented by men only. Cass stubbornly asserted her constitutional rights and practically forced them to allow her to play through. She even took third place in the competition. Another example was with the Lake City Collective School District. The board was looking for free advertising; and, Coven went head-to-head with the chairman of the board explaining just how costly custom advertising is and that Sanderson & Sons couldn't afford to just give it away. She would give them a fair discount and remember not to charge them tax – they were tax-exempt, anyway – but that's as far as she could go. She was quite the bulldog on the part of the agency.

Today, Josie was afraid that bulldog would tear her apart and eat her for lunch. She wasn't far off the mark, as she would soon find out. In the meantime, the staff meeting seemed to drag on and on even though it was in reality shorter than most.

"Let's go have a look at this in my office," Coven said, shaking Josie out of her reverie. "Bring your other ideas with you, too."

They marched down the short hall to the manager's office like it was "The Green Mile"; and, they were on their way to an execution. Josie was scared stiff it was her own execution. She stood near Cass' desk to explain the animated scenes that popped up on the screen before them, too antsy to sit anyway. When it was over, Josie finally sunk into the soft sofa nearby.

"As I tried to explain earlier," Josie started as Cass turned ominously toward her, "that section where the character turns inside out and the action that follows was tricky to show on poster board. I wasn't sure Hildy could do it on the computer. I wanted to be sure before I showed you …" Josie trailed off, noting the proverbial dark clouds rolling in over Cass' head.

"The work is fine," Cass bit out. "You should not have worried about what Hildy can or can't do. You should have trusted her abilities or allowed me to decide if it was worth pursuing. I understand she spent a good half hour on this project – one, that I told you to do. I am extremely disturbed by your lack of teamwork, Josie. I will have to give this matter some serious thought."

Every word that came out of Coven's mouth was laced with disdain. Hatred may have even described it. It took on a physical form that struck Josie stiff with fear. She could feel her heart throbbing in her throat and perspiration forming in each and every gland along the surface of her skin. She caught her breath and sucked air, trying desperately to keep from crying.

"I'm really so-sorry; I-I didn't think it was such a b-big deal," Josie pleaded. "I didn't think she'd get carried away and d-do the whole thing. Honest. I-I just wanted help with one little spot."

"If you need help with anything, my door is always open. It's not your call to go running off to anyone else

Chapter Four
Plan B

Josie was so upset; she nearly forgot her 11:00 appointment. She buzzed Donna on the intercom and asked her to reschedule it for her. She told the receptionist to explain to the client that Josie had come down with a migraine and had to see him tomorrow at 8 a.m. or 4:30 p.m. instead. More choices. Sometimes the choices were inadequate. Sometimes they were downright deadly. Josie was learning the hard way that some choices in life were more than unfair even though they seemed harmless when first offered.

As she snatched a tissue from the floral box on the corner of her desk, Josie thought about the office she could have moved into when she had been promoted to Creative Director. This would have been an excellent time to have the comforting cover of four walls that the office would have proffered. Josie had refused moving into the office for private reasons. She was afraid that very coverage would shield Cass while she stole even more ideas. Because of this, Josie was forced to come up with the lame excuse that she was currently overloaded with projects and didn't have time to make the move. Ah, well, hind sight is 20/20, as they say.

Josie was staring blankly at the snow white story board lying bleakly in front of her when the intercom beeped. Cass was summoning her to her doom. Not wanting to keep her waiting, Josie leaped up and tore down the hall without verbally acknowledging the page.

"Sit down," Coven ordered. Josie plunked down on the couch. "I have thought long and hard about how to handle this insubordination."

Josie cringed at the harsh term. She didn't feel her actions warranted such a drastic description. It was not her intention to be insubordinate. Keeping her eyes lowered and her lips bit shut, Josie waited for the ax to fall.

"Remembering the company policy to allow three black marks on your record before being fired, I have decided to put a written warning in your employee file," Coven stated. "It constitutes one black mark. It should stand as a constant reminder of the chain of command in this organization. Do I make myself clear?"

"Yes, Mam," Josie said meekly.

"Good. Then this will never happen again," Coven commanded as she extended two sheets of paper toward Josie. "This original copy of the reprimand will be placed in your file. Sign it on the bottom line. The other is your copy. Always remember what it means. And, in case you're not clear on that, it means anyone of us can be replaced in a heart beat. None of us is irreplaceable. Consider yourself lucky I didn't find this breach of protocol strong enough to fire you immediately."

Josie left Coven's office in a daze. How could one little action bring about such devastating results? She couldn't fathom the intense response Cass had to one innocent little mistake. Josie was vaguely aware of sitting down at her desk, her head brimming with questions, finding no answers. Her body was numb. How she managed to sit down without missing the chair was a minor miracle.

From that point on, Josie vowed to find another job. She couldn't bear being submitted to that kind of raking over the coals. Josie left the office soon after Coven did. She told Donna her migraine had gotten worse; and, she was going home for the rest of the day. The receptionist didn't answer her, but gave her an inquisitive eye as she made note of it.

Josie didn't go straight home, though. She didn't feel up to fielding questions from her grandmother. There was simply no way to voice a description of what had happened in her boss's office this morning. There was no sane way to explain why Cass had flown off the handle like that. Josie opted to drive down by the lake. There, she was able to watch school children skating, laughing and having snowball fights. Josie sat numbly in her cherry red Mustang, with the motor running until the children were called back to class.

Today was the day of the week when Coven drove 60 miles south into New York City to make contact with her regular clients. Josie nosed her Mustang out of the lakeside parking lot and headed north to Deer Valley. Her stomach was churning and needed something solid to hold down what little breakfast it still contained. Deer Valley had a busy little coffee shop that offered the best chicken dumpling soup in the area. A bowl of that would certainly hit the spot. Josie followed the soup with a huge slice of homemade pumpkin pie a la mode, then drifted down the snowy street to the community library.

She couldn't concentrate on any lengthy novel; however, she did find a couple of interesting women's magazines on the rack. Sitting down at one of the half dozen wooden tables provided for patron use, Josie listlessly paged through the periodicals. Suddenly, she stopped mid-page turn. There was a vividly colored western ad for a major brand of cigarettes. On the adjoining page was a slinky blonde draped over the hood of some extravagantly priced sports car. The model's dress was the same shiny strawberry the car was painted. Red sells. Sex sells.

Red satin, hmmm, Josie thought. She pulled a miniature sketch pad from its everyday pocket in her purse. Fumbling for a pencil, her mind was already awhirl with flowing scarlet satin, bolts and bolts of it streaming across the page with her latest client's product nestled in the center of it.

Hours later, Josie glanced up at the clock above the check-out desk. It was 4:30 already! It was time to go home. She packed up her new creations and headed for the door.

At home, Josie paged through the mail her grandmother had left on the table in the entry. Several return letters had finally arrived from the places she had sent resumes. Not taking time to find the letter opener, Josie tore into each of them. One by one, Josie read rejections of one sort or another. Many had no openings at this time, but would keep her resume on file. A few said she had missed the deadline and/or they had hired someone else. After reading the first couple of informative lines, Josie dropped each one into the trash can standing near the table. She heaved a huge sigh. Of course, she hadn't expected an interview from every one of them, but one offer would have been encouraging.

That's when she noticed the light blinking on the answering machine. The mail had all but covered the little gadget until it had been removed. Pressing the play button, Josie crossed her fingers, then slid out of her coat and turned to hang it on the coat rack near the door.

"Good afternoon, Josie Buchannon!" a masculine voice boomed. "This is Dana Garvey from Garvey, Sloan and Associates in New York City. I received your resume, and while we don't have any permanent positions open at this time, we do have a secretary going on maternity leave in a month or two. The next time you are down this way, please stop by for an interview. I think we have a lot to talk about.

You have our address and phone number. Have a great day!"

Josie whirled about and pressed the play button again. She couldn't believe her ears. Garvey, Sloan and Associates was the best in the business; and, Garvey wanted an interview with her! That bit of news quickly turned her frown upside down and lifted the cloud of despair that had hovered overhead the entire day.

Just then Eleanor Buchannon slid through the kitchen door into the hallway.

"Did you hear that, Gran?" Josie asked excitedly. "Dana Garvey wants to interview me!"

"Well, why shouldn't he?" Josie's Gram asked as she wiped her hands on the paisley printed cobbler's apron she wore over her neat teal blouse and slacks. "You are a talented and educated young woman. My question is, what in the world gave him the idea you were looking for a job? And, by the way, what were all those envelopes from other advertising agencies all about? Come with me into the kitchen. You can tell me what all this is about over a cup of hot tea; Earl Gray or apple cinnamon?"

Eleanor Buchannon liked to use a little old-fashioned herbal medicine to soothe some hurts. This seemed like a good time to break out the family remedy.

"I had sensed something was up at work – all the extra projects you were bringing home on weekends and evenings," Eleanor told her granddaughter, "but, I never suspected it to be that bad. Just what is going on, Josie?"

Josie sat down at the kitchen table and waited for her grandmother to put the kettle on to boil before she answered. When Eleanor sat down across the table from her, Josie heaved a heavy sigh before plunging into her tale.

"My boss seems to be a power crazy dictator with delusions of godhood!" she blurted. "I needed help with a project she wanted to see before going to the production person to finish it off. The problem was a production technicality, so I asked Hildy if she could pull off with her computer what I had in mind. Well, she took my whole project and spent a half hour finishing it. When I presented it to Cass, she nearly blew a gasket. I think she liked how it turned out, but she was so furious that I took it to Hildy first that she nearly fired me."

"Yes, I can see where that would seem like a threat to someone who is insecure about their authority," Grams agreed. The tea kettle whistled; and, she stood up to reach it. After pouring the scalding hot water into the prepared tea cups, she placed the pot back on the stove. Josie twirled her apple cinnamon tea bag in the steaming cup without saying a word.

"When did you find time to prepare and send out your resume? What made you decide to do that before this scene took place this morning?" Grams asked.

"About a month ago – around the time I was promoted to Creative Director -- I was suspicious of Cass. I thought she was stealing my ideas," Josie confessed. "We kept coming up with many of the same ideas; and, I was getting frustrated. So, I gave her a few off-the-cuff ideas. She ran with them, taking credit for them as well. I took your advice to hope for the best but prepare for the worst. I developed most of my ideas at home and copied them to disks to carry with me instead of emailing them to the office. I haven't left any projects on my desk either, unless I wanted them to show up on Cass's idea list. I even rearranged my schedule so it would take me out of the office during the times Cass was scheduled to be in. That way I wouldn't have to sit down in a planning session with her where she could pick my brain for campaigns she could take credit for by beating me to the punch. If she noticed I was avoiding her, she never said anything. But it really came to a head this morning."

Grams let Josie's story sink in before she said anything. She knew that sometimes just having someone to tell your woes to helped clear the cobwebs and sooth wounded hearts.

"Anyway, Grams, at least I have a lead if things do get any worse," Josie said with more cheerfulness than she actually felt. "I'm sorry I didn't tell you about this earlier. I had built it up in my mind to be this horrible problem that only I could handle. I didn't want to bother you."

"Nonsense, child," Grams purred. "Grandmothers have been helping granddaughters solve their lives' crises for centuries, even if it means just pouring tea and listening." The two women smiled at each other. Love emanated from both faces.

"Not to dispel the comfort of the moment," Grams hedged, "but just what are you going to do now?"

Chapter Five
Pushing the Envelope

Just what was she going to do now? Josie was struck with the enormity of the question. She had told her grandmother she would try to stick it out for a few more months. Staying in one job for a full year meant a great deal to future employers. She had explained to Grams just how much working in her home town and living with her grandmother meant to her. However, they both agreed that if one was unhappy with their work environment, it had a negative effect on her production. It seemed like a no-win scenario.

At least, Josie thought, *I have Dana Garvey's offer to fall back on. The only problem is that position will be filled soon, too. I will have to make my decision in the next couple of weeks, not months.*

When Josie walked into the office the next morning, mousy little Donna Schmidd actually asked her if her headache was gone. It was much better, Josie assured her, and thanked her for her concern. Josie had to look twice as Donna was sporting a nose ring. Huh! That was new – and unexpected.

The thought followed Josie to her desk. "Expect the unexpected" was another axiom that popped into her mind. She surveyed the store front with its herd of desks and realized this had become home to her. Josie sat down and dove into her work. By the end of a long day of trying to please finicky client, Josie had forgotten the axiom.

< * >

That night, while Josie packed it in early – needing a full night's sleep, Cass was entertaining her lover.

"I just had to see you, Lew," Coven crooned. "I know it's not the weekend, but I'm so glad you could come over."

Sanderson helped himself to a splash of bourbon from Coven's wet bar as he contemplated what his petite protégé had up her sleeve tonight. Turning, he saw she had draped herself seductively over the plush white sofa in her living room. She had prepared extensively for this appointment with an aromatherapy bath and a new silk negligee. Her hair was sparkling like it had never shone before. It was a pretty package, Sanderson admitted to himself. If only she were the marrying type.

"Okay, I'll bite," Sanderson said. "Just what do I owe the pleasure of this invitation?"

"Sit down and let me loosen your tie, first," Coven said, practically purring. "You shouldn't have to wear those stuffy pin-striped suits every day. What a pain." She loosened the navy tie that perfectly matched the wool garment Sanderson wore, then unbuttoned the top three buttons of his ice blue shirt and traced circles through his chest hair. She knew that drove him nuts.

"If we're ever going to get to the fun and games," Lew said teasingly, "you'd better come clean, quickly."

"It's just that I had a problem with Josie yesterday. I was ready to fire her," Coven began. She laid her head on his shoulder and continued tracing circles across Lew's chest, working her way downward. "She disobeyed a direct order to run a company promotional idea by me before sending it to production. I was able to intervene before it went any further; but, Lew, it could've been disastrous …"

"I can't believe Josie would deliberately do anything to hurt the agency," Sanderson said before downing the last of his drink and setting the glass on the end table. "Josie is a responsible young woman with a good head on her shoulders. You make it sound like mutiny."

Coven sat up at the use of such a derogatory term. She locked eyes with Sanderson. Coven wasn't sure where he was headed with that; but, in her estimation, the term fit.

"I can't read Josie's mind, Lew; but, when I give a direct order, I expect it to be obeyed," Coven stated flatly. She wasn't about to let him know the exact details. It sounded silly even to her, now that it was over. At the time it happened; though, all Coven could see was red. No underling was going to go behind Cassandra Coven's back and get away with it! And, there was no way Coven would back down now. That would look stupid, weak and incompetent. So, she continued to push the idea that Josie did it out of spite.

"Listen to you, woman!" Sanderson said jovially. "You sound like a drill sergeant in the army. 'Obey me, or else!' Come on, Cassie. Lighten up. You got your revenge with the written warning. Besides, the job market is soft right now. Everyone is hiring, and there won't be any new graduates for several months. You wouldn't be able to replace her as easily as you think. On top of that, you wouldn't match her caliber with a greenhorn; and we can't afford to match big city wages. Let it go. That's enough. I don't want to hear anymore about it, or I won't be in the mood to stay any longer."

"Well, we can't have that!" Coven agreed. She was reluctant to let the stalemate lie; but, she couldn't see any way around it. If she pushed the envelope with this, it might make Lew suspicious enough to get Josie's side of the story.

Then, Cass would be out on her ear. The thought that drifted through Coven's mind, leaving the most frustration, was, *Why was Lew single-mindedly defending Josie?*

In the long run, Coven couldn't afford to rankle Sanderson's suspicions; so, she wisely kept her mouth shut for the rest of the evening, except for the foreplay in which they were now engaged. The smart cookie always knew when to retreat; and Coven wasn't born yesterday. She knew who paid her salary; and, she intended to keep him happy. However, throughout the two-hour love-making session, Coven's mind was divided between the task at hand and the plot she was hatching to force Josie into resigning on her own.

Chapter Six
The Cutting Edge

The next day was Wednesday, "hump day", the middle of the week. The thought kept revolving in Josie's mind. It had been such a trying week; and, it was only half over! She dragged herself out of bed and into the shower. As the hot water beat her back, Josie tried to think of all the reasons why she loved her job and should want to go back to work. The balance sheet seemed tipped in its favor; but, the negative side was that Cass was gunning for her. Every tiny little thing she did would be scrutinized from here on out. Her heart sank. She ended up soaking a little longer than usual to try to pull herself back together. Trudging through the details of make-up and dressing was sheer torture when all she wanted to do was crawl back into bed and pull the covers over her head. The black pant suit Josie pulled from her closet seemed to fit her mood to a T. It was a good thing it was Gram's club day. She had left the house already and wouldn't witness just what bad company Josie would be over breakfast.

In fact, today, I'm skipping breakfast, Josie thought. *What's the use? I won't be needing extra energy after Cass fires me.* With that gloomy thought, she left the house with a wet head, actually looking forward to catching a cold.

Traffic was slow due to the newly fallen snow. By the time Josie reached the office, Cass had left on her appointed rounds. Josie grabbed a cup of hot chocolate from the break room and sat down at her desk to work up the latest story board, one for Mason's Masonry.

Oh, great! She thought. *Just what I needed to complete the mood: an ad for head stones.*

Just then Jessica walked by, swishing her mini skirt and clicking her heals across the floor. Josie glanced up and caught Jessica's eye.

"Is that a new outfit?" Josie tried to be polite. Jessica stopped in front of her desk.

"No, but I do have something new!" Jessica said as she stuck her well-manicured left hand under Josie's nose. "It was my birthday yesterday, you know. Look what Jimmy gave me!"

"Well, congratulations, Jessica! That is terrific," Josie said, grabbing Jessica's hand to hold it still enough to get a good look at the giant rock on the other girl's ring finger. "I didn't realize gas station attendants make this kind of money; but, I'm happy for you. It's a gorgeous ring."

"Thank you, thank you!" Jessica gushed and floated away.

Just what I need, Josie moaned inwardly. *First, grave markers; and, now, co-workers on Cloud Nine. What else is going to happen to me today?*

After a couple of unsuccessful attempts at sketching head stones, Josie decided to take an early lunch. It wasn't that she was hungry – she knew the gnawing feeling in the pit of her stomach was nerves, not hunger – but, she needed a break to clear her head. After informing the receptionist where she was going, Josie strolled across the street to the little home town café without her coat. The icy breeze stroked her senses and filled her lungs with a sharpness that proved she was still alive. By the time she took a booth, it had perked her appetite, as well. Ordering a bacon cheese burger and onion rings suddenly sounded appealing. While she waited for her order, Josie read the funnies in the daily paper and worked on the cross word puzzle. While sipping the chocolate malt she ordered for desert, Josie read the Horoscope.

It said, "You are in danger. Watch your step." Whatever did that mean? How could Josie be in danger in her home town? That must have been a figurative meaning. In that case, it could easily apply to her job situation.

Back at the shop, Josie found notes from her afternoon appointments. They had to reschedule due to the weather. One was snowed in at a ski resort he frequented on weekends. That must've been some weekend, Josie mused. The other's Cherokee pane had been grounded in the next county where she had her private airport. Josie shook her head and faked a frown. Some people have all the advantages. It did occur to her; though, that these people had worked their whole lives for the privileges they enjoyed. She simply wondered if she, herself, would ever be so fortunate as to have paid enough dues to enjoy similar privileges.

Josie was hard at work on yet another story board when Cass blew in with the wind. Coven always made an entrance, blonde business women always did; but, the winter wind was at her back and literally drove her into the building with gusto.

"Whoooooeeee!" Coven exclaimed. "That wind is picking up! Donna, you had better head home before you don't make it home!" Then she snatched up her messages and whisked her petite form down the office isles like some western tornado. She paused long enough at the production booth to repeat her order to Hildy. When she got to Jessica's cubby, she reminded the researcher that this was her day to leave early. Even though Jessica lived in town, Coven didn't want to see her stuck in the snow bank trying to flag down nonexistent traffic in that micro-mini skirt she had on. Moving on toward her office she nearly passed Josie without saying a word; but, stopped short one step beyond the Creative Director's desk.

"Josie, you usually work late on Wednesdays, right? And, with you living just a few blocks away, would you mind taking out the garbage before you leave?" Coven asked innocently. "I have a doctor's appointment over in Deer Valley this afternoon; and, with the weather as it is, I probably won't make it back in time to catch the garbage truck. Be a dear and do that for me, will you?"

Coven left for her office without even waiting for a reply. Josie sat there with her mouth gaping open while everyone else pulled on their coats and headed for the door. She was so flabbergasted at the thought of being taken for granted; she didn't even return the good-night greetings the others tossed her way. Within minutes, Coven flew out of her office with her briefcase and a determined look on her face. Sparks seemed to fly from her icy green eyes.

"Drive carefully!" Josie forced the unfelt sentiment passed her clenched teeth. Coven breezed on by her without acknowledging her effort at civility. Then, suddenly, Josie was alone, abandoned in the all-too quiet business office. Not even the telephones rang. All the other ladies must have called their significant others to tell them of their early departure.

"That reminds me," Josie said to herself, "I had better call Grams to see if she's all right. I'll ask her if she needs any groceries or prescriptions. You just don't know when weather like this can keep you trapped in your house for a few days."

Dialing her home phone number, Josie made a list of basic food stuffs Grams might ask her to bring home, then pulled her black wool blazer closer to her body for warmth. With everyone leaving in a stampede, the draft created by the open door chilled the air and tickled Josie's nose. Grams didn't need anything as she had stopped by the store on her way home from club. She just wanted Josie to stay safe and warm, not stay too late at work.

The afternoon wore on; the clouds darkened the sky more quickly than the early-setting winter sun. Shadows crept along the floor and up the walls as Josie labored over her work. Finally, it was close to 5:00 p.m. She looked up only to notice how dark it was outside.

Darker than dark, she thought. It was time to go home. *OOPS!* She had better not forget the garbage. With no cleaning staff on the payroll (saving on the budget), Coven had taken over those duties. She had collected the trash that morning before leaving on her rounds. The huge, stuffed plastic sack was setting near the back door. All Josie had to do was drag it outside and let it set on the back steps. After organizing her purse and briefcase to go home, Josie slipped into her coat and headed toward the back door.

Snap, she flipped the switch to turn on the outdoor light to illuminate the steps. Nothing. The light bulb must have burned out. Shrugging her shoulders, Josie hefted the bulging sack and pulled open the door. Stepping over the threshold and turning right, she gingerly lowered the bag onto the small platform that served as a break area for smokers as well as the garbage pick-up area.

As she straightened up, Josie felt a band of steel wrap around her chest, pinning her arms. Josie went frigid, her head tilting upward and her eyes bulging out. Was some neighborhood kid playing a practical joke on her?

In the darkness, a cold, steel edge slid at an angle toward Josie's neck. She continued to hold very still as the sharp edge of a butcher knife played along her Adam's apple. Josie was paralyzed with fear.

"Leave town forever or feel the cutting edge," growled a mysterious voice. Then, as suddenly as the intruder had appeared, he or she leapt from the steps and disappeared around the back of the building.

It was too dark; and, the figured moved too swiftly for Josie to recognize it. When the footsteps receded, Josie thawed enough to sidle inside and lock the door behind her. Heaving gulps of air like a drowning victim, Josie tore off to the front of the office to lock the front door. Then, she rushed to her desk and dialed 911.

"Help! Help!" Josie screamed when the switchboard operator answered her call. "I've been attacked at knifepoint!"

"Calm down, miss," the dispatcher said. "What is your name and where are you calling from?"

Giving the officer all the details as rationally as she could, Josie took her advice and started taking deep breaths as soon as she was finished with the information relay. The dispatcher kept trying to assure Josie everything was going to be all right. Had she locked the doors? Was she bleeding and needed an ambulance?

Josie's free hand flew to her desk drawer where she kept a pocket-sized mirror. She lifted it out and peered into it. Her neck, while visibly scraped, was not bleeding. She would live. On the other hand, her face was as white as the new snow outside. She had never been this frightened before. She caught herself laughing. *It must be frayed nerves,* she thought.

Just then, she heard a knock at the front door. It was the deputy. She could see him holding a flashlight on himself for her benefit.

"The deputy has arrived," Josie told the operator. "Thank you so, so much for being there for me!"

"That's my job," the dispatcher replied. "I'm happy to serve you. Good-bye."

Josie ran to the front door and let the officer in. He introduced himself as Deputy Clements. She led him into the office area and babbled her story, not sure if she made any sense.

"My partner went around back to take a look," Clements reported. "Unfortunately, with the fresh, blowing snow, I don't think he will find anything. Do you think you will make it home all right?"

"If you walk me to my car and see me off," Josie said weakly, nodding her head. "I don't want to scare Grams by riding up in a squad car; but, maybe you could follow me home and just keep an eye on me to make sure I get into the house safely."

The officer agreed and waited while Josie called her grandmother just to let her know she was on her way. That way, Josie could assure herself that Grams was all right, too.

Clements' partner met them at the front door, shaking his head negatively. It was just as Clements had predicted: no clues because of the weather. They inspected Josie's neck quickly before ushering her through the door and locking it. They agreed they could just barely see a scrape mark along the middle of her throat. Clements put an arm around Josie to help her to her car while his partner took down some notes for their report. They didn't leave the side of her Mustang until she was ready to pull away from the curb.

"Call us if the intruder shows up again," they chimed, handing her their business card. She cranked the window shut against the icy wind and drove home.

Chapter Seven
The Big Move

That cinched it! Josie couldn't stay at Sanderson & Sons any longer. Her life had just been threatened. If the perpetrator knew her well enough to find her at work, she or he may very well know where Josie lives, making Grams a prospective victim as well. Josie wouldn't be able to live with herself if she was the cause of anything terrible happening to her grandmother. Unfortunately, this was not something she could keep from Grams, either. As soon as she got home, Josie vowed she would tell her grandmother everything.

Once she had thawed out over a cup of hot chocolate, Josie revealed to her grandmother the reason she was late. Grams was appropriately shocked and grateful Josie wasn't hurt or killed. Yes, of course, Josie should call Dana Garvey first thing in the morning to take him up on his offer. It would give her an immediate income while she looked for an apartment and a permanent job. Grams would stay here and hold down the fort. Someone had to keep an eye on the house and pretend nothing happened. She would also call the sheriff's department on Josie's behalf and see if they couldn't keep her name out of the crime news. Perhaps the investigators would welcome a chance to let the perpetrator show himself again so they could get more clues.

"The cops would keep an eye on me," Grams assured Josie. "They won't let anything happen to me."

Remembering the police patrol on their street, Josie was finally able to get some sleep that night.

While she slept, 10 inches of snow were dumped on the dwellings of Lake City. It continued to snow the next morning. Josie awoke late due to the overcast shadows on her bedroom wall. She had never needed an alarm clock before; but, today, it would have been useful. Surely, no one made it to the office; but she had to try to contact her co-workers to let them know she wasn't coming in today.

Sliding into her bedroom slippers and quilted bathrobe, Josie padded down the stairs and into the kitchen. Grams had been up for hours and was keeping a kettle warm for Josie as she read yesterday's paper. Today's edition would be late for certain.

"Good morning, Pussycat," Grams said, greeting Josie with her childhood nickname. "How are you feeling this morning?"

"A little better, Grams," Josie said and realized it was true. She smiled. "You look good in that lavender pants and sweater set. Isn't that the one I gave you for Christmas?"

"Yes, it is, dear. Thank you. Have a seat while I dish up your breakfast," Grams said. "So, what are you going to do today, seeing as how we can't get out of the house?"

Josie pulled out her usual chair and plopped down on it. She fixed her grandmother with a solemn look and pursed her lips. Grams set the oatmeal dish in front of Josie and mimicked the studied stare. Then they both broke out laughing.

"Well, first, I want to call Mr. Garvey and set an interview," Josie said between bites. "I just haven't decided how much I should tell Cass in my letter of resignation, which I'll probably have to E-mail today. Should I make something up? I know even if I could hand it to her in person, she would still walk me to the door immediately and write me off. It may not be the most professional way to resign, but considering the weather isn't being cooperative, I don't have a whole lot of choice in the matter, And, it will save me that embarrassment."

"Do what you have to do, dear," Grams said, being supportive. "If there's anything I can help you with – packing, laundry, phone calls – just say the word. I'm at your disposal today."

They both chuckled at that. Of course, neither one of them were going anywhere until the city crew dug them out; and, Josie was feeling pretty secure in the fact that the attacker from the night before wouldn't be after her in weather like this. That would be insane! So, she and her grandmother spent the remainder of the day packing Josie's suitcases and playing board games. After lunch, Josie tried calling the office; but, there was no answer. Since she didn't like leaving loose ends, Josie composed a letter of resignation to send to Cass's work and home computers and printed it out to send a hard copy with her actual signature on it as well. She didn't want Cass claiming Josie just didn't show up for work one day.

In her letter of resignation, Josie made it clear that she was offered a better job in New York (she didn't mention where), and that she had to leave immediately in order to take it. She also spelled out the fact that she believed Cass would have walked her to the door the day she received the letter whether or not Josie gave her two weeks' notice, so it came out the same in the end. She wished Sanderson & Sons Advertising Agency a prosperous New Year without her. Josie really did care that the company survived, even thrived. She just wished Mr. Sanderson knew just how crudely his manager was managing his business. That was a real disappointment to her, Josie realized as she sealed the envelope to be mailed.

< * >

Josie never heard a peep from the staff at Sanderson & Sons after that day. She assumed Cass had turned them against her; and, they went on with their lives without missing her one bit. She would just have to do the same, she thought, as she headed her red sports car down the freeway toward the Big Apple Friday morning.

Grams had packed her a picnic basket full of sandwiches, bars and apples, and a thermos of hot tea. She said tea was healthier than hot chocolate and easier to transport than something Josie liked to gob whipped cream on top. Josie listened to the local radio station long enough to catch the area news. The crime slot was extremely short today. No mention of her attack was made; so, Josie popped in a cassette tape of her favorite artist, Reba McIntyre.

"I am a survivor," the Country Music icon belted out. Josie thought that was a fitting little ditty for this trip and lost herself in thoughts of her new job and her new life.

Chapter Eight
The Big Apple

Driving straight to the YWCA nearest the address given for Garvey, Sloan and Associates, LTD, Josie took a parking spot as close to the main entrance as possible. She was hoping she wouldn't have to move her vehicle in order to unload the few belongings she would take in with her. The clerk gave her a key and directions to her assigned room in exchange for a week's rent. It was only $100.00, but without a definite job, that money looked mighty valuable to Josie. She paid it and snatched the key to her temporary new home. She would find an apartment after she found a permanent job.

It didn't take long for her to haul her suitcase, pillow and quilt to the tiny box of a room. Looking around the 10' X 10' cell, Josie was glad she hadn't packed up a U-Haul with all her furniture, too. The single bed took up most of one wall and half the floor. There was a desk and chair under the window and the closet took up the third wall. There was an antique stuffed arm chair behind the door. Apparently, the Y expected renters to take their meals elsewhere as there was no sign of a microwave, refrigerator or anything else food-related.

At least it's clean, Josie thought, dropping her pillow and quilt onto the bed then slid the suitcase onto the table.

As she unpacked and hung up her work suits in the space provided, Josie thought about ways to make this room reflect the occupant. The quilt Grams had made for her was the only trademark so far. Fishing in the bottom of her suitcase, she brought out a framed picture of her grandmother and herself. She placed it on the desk behind the suitcase, promising to buy a potted plant to set next to it. Once the unpacking was done, Josie took her cell phone out of her purse and dialed home.

"Grams, I'm here!" Josie said as soon as her grandmother picked up on her end. "I'm at the Y that I gave you the number for. Of course, you can call my cell phone, too. That would be easiest."

"I'm glad you arrived safely, dear!" Her grandmother's voice reached her through the telephone. It felt like a verbal hug to Josie. "Good luck in your interview later. Love you!"

"Thanks, Grams. I needed that," Josie said. "Love you, too. Good-bye!"

With that, Josie changed into her best navy suit with the crisp white linen blouse and matching navy pumps and earrings. She pulled her shoulder-length chestnut hair into a knot at the back of her neck and checked her pantyhose for runs. On the way out the door, Josie said a little prayer for a productive interview and jumped into her trusty car.

Here we go, she thought, and drove away.

< * >

The advertising agency of Garvey, Sloan and Associates took up half an entire city block. Josie stood outside her car in the employee parking lot that used up the other half of the block and spilled into the next. Her gaze drifted up and down the reflective glass tiles that blanketed the crystalline structure, its aqua tint reminiscent of her zircon birthstone.

Josie's breath caught in her throat. She gulped once, twice. Looking at the huge corporation from the outside dwarfed Josie's self confidence. Imagining what it looked like on the inside made her feel about two inches tall.

"Well, it's now or never," she said, pinching herself. "Get in there and get it over with." She picked up her portfolio and, mustering all the grace and posture she could, marched across the parking lot and into the main door.

Both receptionists were occupied with speaking on hands-free headsets and tapping keys on inset computer terminals. Josie set her portfolio on the ledge of the desk and drew a deep breath. She spun a slow 360 to take in the mezzanine. Then, looking upward into the skylight nine stories high, Josie experienced a spinning wooziness that could only have been vertigo. She reached out with her right hand and grasped the edge of the receptionists' desk to steady herself.

"May I help you?" the receptionist on the right asked. Josie jerked her head downward and away from the dizzying sight above.

"Uh, yes," she answered. She squinted, trying to focus on the spot where the voice had come from. "I'm here to see Mr. Dana Garvey. I am Josephine Buchannon."

"Josephine Buchannon," the ebony beauty repeated. "Yes, here you are; right on time, too. Take the elevator to your left up to the top floor and go straight to the end of the hall. Mrs. Colson is Mr. Garvey's executive assistant. She will help you from there."

"Thanks," Josie said as she picked up her portfolio. Turning left, she forced herself to cross the floor to a shaft of four elevators. Entering a waiting cubicle, she pushed the button marked "9" and stepped to the rear of the car.

Breathe, she told herself, *breathe*. Unfortunately, the car shot up at such a speed as to take her breath away. She lurched forward and stuck out a hand to keep herself from ramming into the sliding doors. She could just imagine riding in this fashion every morning. It was definitely a good thing she hadn't had breakfast, for it would have been all over the floor by now. The car stopped as suddenly as it had started and nearly bounced her out the doors as they zipped open. Smoothing her hair and collecting her wits, she headed toward the far end of the hall, as per direction, passing dozens of work cubicles.

"Mrs. Colson?" Josie inquired at the open corner desk. The lady seated there was the epitome of perfection in Josie's book. Her impeccable slate tweed suit and bouffant hairdo left no mistake this woman was a professional business woman.

"Yes. Can I help you?" Mrs. Colson replied.

"Josie Buchannon," Josie introduced herself. "I have an interview with Mr. Garvey in …" she consulted her watch … "ten minutes?"

"Of course," Mrs. Colson said, leaving her desk and leading Josie to a waiting area. "I'll take your coat and you can take a seat over here. I will let Mr. Garvey know you are here. I'm sure he will be with you in just a minute."

"Thank you," Josie said. She felt like she was on auto pilot. It's a good thing those two little words were in her vocabulary. They fit a zillion situations and are commonly accepted worldwide. She took a seat and pulled out a pocket mirror to check her appearance. Not a hair was out of place in spite of the rocket ride. She licked her lips and slid the mirror back in to her pocket, and then patted her portfolio as if it were a faithful dog.

Mrs. Colson suddenly reappeared saying Mr. Garvey would see her now. Josie picked up her portfolio and followed her guide into a spacious corner office. Windows lined two walls and bookshelves covered everything else except the door. Josie had never seen such an enormous work area for one person. It was so huge, the leather sofa sat in the middle of the room without touching a wall. Mrs. Colson introduced Josie to a sharp-looking middle-aged man in a black pin-striped suit with salt-and-pepper hair to match. A little bowtie of a mustache feathered his top lip which drew the bottom lip with it into a broad smile.

"Pleased to meet you, Mr. Garvey," Josie managed to say. She reached out to shake his hand; and, he met her half way with a vice grip.

"I have been looking forward to meeting you, Miss Buchannon," the man replied. "When I read your resume, I said to myself, I couldn't afford to let you slip away. Please, have a seat on the couch. It will take the formality out of our appointment."

"Please call me 'Josie'," she said as she sat down. Mr. Garvey sat in a velvet captain's chair set perpendicular to the sofa. He crossed his legs and rested his chin on his thumb as he gazed at her.

"Okay, Josie. I like that. Perhaps after you've worked here a while, you can call me by my first name," he said, then chuckled. "Everyone I know calls me Mr. Garvey, except my wife and my mother."

Josie couldn't help smirking a little. If this was a ply to help her relax, it was working. "So, tell me something about yourself that isn't on your resume," Mr. Garvey requested.

"Well, Josie began; and, stopped to clear her throat. "I'm loyal, punctual and trustworthy. I was raised by my grandmother after my mother died in childbirth. I grew up in Lake City and have lived with Grams all this time. My work has been published in various magazines and even on our local television channel. Um, I'm also available to start work Monday, due to circumstances beyond my control."

"How is that?" the agency president asked. "Did you get fired?"

"No; although, with the way things were going, I wouldn't have put it passed Cass to have fired me," Josie admitted. "She and I weren't on the best of terms because I was trying to avoid having her steal my ad ideas. I was there nearly a year; and I would have tried to stay longer; but, I had – a – little run-in with someone …"

"Just what kind of 'run-in'?" Garvey asked. "You don't seem to be the type of person that would deliberately cause trouble."

Josie shifted in her seat. This wasn't going to be easy. It was becoming crystal clear she would have to tell this man everything if she had any hopes of him hiring her.

"Okay, this is what happened. Wednesday night, Cass asked me to take out the trash for her. She had let the cleaning lady go and had been doing that job, herself, Well, she had a doctor's appointment in Deer Valley and didn't think she would make it back due to the weather."

Josie went on to tell the whole heart-stopping story. Garvey sat there listening and nodding. He made Josie feel comfortable with the way he seemed to believe her. When she was finished, she felt relieved. She glanced up at her prospective employer in hopeful anticipation. He didn't let her down. However, he did surprise her with his next comment.

"Do you think your boss may have been the attacker?" he asked. I've met Cassandra Coven. We were at the same advertising convention last fall. I was not impressed. She was underdressed and overbearing. Once, when I tried to turn away to talk to someone else, she grabbed my arm. That woman is stronger than she looks. She must work out. I also got the impression she would do anything to get her way. And, I do mean *anything*."

Josie sat up bolt-right. She hadn't given that a thought. She knew Cass was devious enough to steal her ideas, but she hadn't suspected she was capable of such a deadly threat. She sat back, closing her eyes, trying to remember any little detail she may have missed when talking to the deputies.

"Perfume," she mumbled and opened her eyes. "Yes! Now, I remember the scent of sultry perfume. I had been in shock before and didn't remember that. But, now that I think about it, there was a hint of perfume. And – cigarette smoke. Now, why didn't I remember that before? I suppose I assumed there would be cigarette smoke out there because that's where Cass takes her cigarette breaks. The office is a smoke-free environment. That's good, because I'm allergic to smoke. Then again, with the wind blowing the way it was, there shouldn't have been any smoke out there anymore. It had been early morning since Cass had been out there. So, it had to have been on her coat."

"Anything else?" Garvey prodded.

"Actually, I didn't think much of it at the time; but, there was something else," Josie said. She shook her head up and down, biting her bottom lip. "There was a stump on the steps right behind me. I nearly tripped on it as I edged back inside. It is used as a chair; but, it normally sets further off to the side, not smack dab in the middle of the porch. That must be what she was standing on to get a good angle at my throat. Cass is nearly a foot shorter than me!"

"Exactly," Garvey commented. "Now you have more information you can share with your sheriff's department. And, a great reason to leave your former employer for a safer work environment. None of that actually proves it was Coven; but, it should ease your mind that you are moving in the right direction. Now, let's see that portfolio."

The two of them poured over Josie's work for nearly an hour. Garvey noted that half the finished work had Cass's by-line on it. Josie defended herself by reminding him Cass had been taking credit for her ideas.

"Oh, I believe you," he said. "I can see the consistency between your work and the ads she claimed she did. I could see that the moment I moved from one to the next. You are quite talented for someone who didn't actually major in advertising. No, that's quite all right, Josie. you don't need to get defensive. What I have in mind for you will utilize the best of both worlds. you will have an opportunity to use your business management degree and get some copy time in as well."

"How so?" she asked, not quite believing her ears. "I thought the position you had open was a temporary secretarial slot."

Mr. Garvey tilted his head, sporting a little devilish smile. He kept her in suspense for just a moment.

"Yes, you will start out in the secretarial pool. It will allow you to get to know your way around the office. However, that position will be open six to eight weeks, tops. Mary Ellen Peterson plans to return after having her baby," Garvey continued, toying with Josie's curiosity. "In fact, her position is only part-time."

"Now, wait just a minute," Josie interrupted, flushing with anger. Was this guy just leading her on? "You never said anything about it being part-time, just temporary. I can't afford to even live at the Y if it's just a part-time job."

"Tut! Tut!" Garvey said, raising his hand to stop her tirade. "The other half the day, I want you shadowing myself and/or Mr. Mark Tuttle. Mr. Tuttle is the Accounting Manager. He is also in charge of all Accounts Payable, including payroll. He is scheduled to retire in two months."

"That sounds like a bigger position," Josie demurred, "but how does advertising fit in with cutting checks?"

"Only because I say it does," Garvey said cryptically. "My partner, Jacob Sloan, and I have been racking our brains trying to come up with new advertising for our own company. All our account execs are tied up with their own clients; none of them have time to work on it. I figured with your fresh perspective, you could come up with something innovative and futuristic. There may be other projects in the future we can use you on as well. So, what do you think? Does that sound challenging enough for you? Are you in?"

Chapter Nine
New York: New Opportunities

Mr. Garvey had just asked Josie if she wanted the job he had just outlined for her.

"We-ell," Josie drawled. "Since I don't have anything pressing to do for the next couple of months, I guess it wouldn't hurt to give it a try."

The two shook hands on the deal, then Garvey turned Josie back over to Mrs. Colson for paperwork and a company tour. He also asked her to give Josie a hand finding better living quarters. Colson set Josie down at her own desk to complete 35 minutes worth of employment forms while she went to lunch. She brought back a chicken salad sandwich and a diet soda for the company's newest employee, as well as an offer to rent her the apartment above her garage.

Armed with a map, directions, address and telephone number of her new abode, Josie floated out of the building. Once in her car, she pulled out her cell phone and called her grandmother.

"Grams! I got the job!" She practically shouted over the airway. "In fact, it's better than I imagined."

"Good for you, girl! I knew you would get it," Grams replied, congratulated Josie, and then asked for some details.

"That temporary secretarial position is only half-time," Josie began. "The other half the time I will be training for the position of Accounts Payable manager! Mr. Garvey was pretty crafty with his description of the job. That sly fox had me going there for a while about a part-time temporary job in the secretarial pool. He had me worried for a spell. And, oh! Grams, get a pen and paper. Mr. Garvey's assistant is letting me rent the apartment above her garage. I have the address here."

When she finished relaying the information to her grandmother, Josie said good-bye without mentioning the facts surrounding the attack that Mr. Garvey helped her remember. She pulled out the card Deputy Clements had given her that terrifying night, three days ago, and quickly dialed his direct line. Clements was out of the office; but, she left the new data on his voice mail. With that task out of the way, she drove back to the YWCA to collect her things.

After reloading her car, Josie headed to the front desk to turn in her key and inquire as to a refund. It wasn't in the Y's policy to give refunds; however, since she hadn't even spent one night there, the registration clerk gave back half her deposit. Well, that would help stock her shelves with groceries, Josie thought as she headed back to the parking lot.

Since the directions Mrs. Colson gave her were from the agency, Josie decided the safest route to take would be to start from there. It wasn't that far away; but, she could easily end up in Brooklyn if she didn't drive back to Garvey, Sloan and Associates first. New York was no place to get lost in, she reminded herself. Besides, another look at her new job site was pleasing to the eye. The directions were detailed and easy to follow. Josie found herself pulling up next to a chalk white colonial-style home with a three-car garage hidden in the back. She pulled into the driveway and parked in front of the nearest garage door. Just as Mrs. Colson had explained, there was a sidewalk leading around to the opposite side where a wooden staircase lead to the second floor apartment.

"This is great!" Josie said to no one but her shadow as she let herself in with the key Mrs. Colson had given her. The two-room apartment reminded her of a lake cabin she had stayed in as a kid. The walls were wood grain paneling with chintz curtains. The furniture was second hand; but, in good shape. She waltzed around the main room taking in the kitchenette that was separated from the living room by the back of the sofa. There was even a television set perched on an antique steamer trunk. Down the short hall, Josie found the bedroom held a double bed, a dresser and an armoire. Across the hall was a full-sized bathroom with shower stall. The décor was somewhat masculine, reflecting Colson's oldest son's tastes. Josie had been told it was he that had renovated the place as a college project.

After the initial inspection, it didn't take Josie long to unload her car and unpack her sparse belongings one more time. Flipping on the TV, she sat down to make a shopping list. Mrs. Colson had also given her directions to the nearest 7-11 where she could pick up a few things to tide her over. Josie was promised a full tour and grocery store trip the following day. She couldn't get over how helpful Mrs. Colson was and couldn't imagine her going this far out of her way for just anyone.

While Josie contemplated her grocery needs, a computer commercial popped on the television screen. It boasted of personal service and tailored products. Josie ceased writing to observe the advertisement. The computer company didn't show any space-age technology other than the computer, itself. It didn't make any promises other than giving customers only what they need without sky-high prices.

Interesting concept, Josie thought. Most vendors push to sell more – more buttons, more gadgets, more everything, resulting in more money spent. However, in a down or fluctuating economy, the common person tends to be conservative, looking to reduce, reuse and/or recycle. They want to get a few extra miles out of the vehicle or equipment they have without spending an arm and a leg on upgrades. Josie made a couple of notes, promising herself to compare this company's commitments with the services and philosophy of Garvey, Sloan and Associates. The results of that bit of research might provide a little background for her new assignment.

After the trip to the local convenience store and shelving her purchases, Josie sat down at the table in the tiny kitchenette with a cup of vegetable beef soup and her sketch pad and colored charcoal set. She had turned on the television, again, for company, some background noise to fill the void while she doodled. Before long, the activities of the day caught up with her; she yawned. Stretching, Josie got up to check the lock on the door. She found a chain lock as well as the key entry and slid the knob into place. Feeling secure in her new surroundings, Josie slept soundly until the sun woke her the next morning.

True to her word, Mrs. Colson called for Josie at 11 a.m. to take her out to lunch and tour the town. Josie had showered and pulled on charcoal wool slacks and a pastel pink turtleneck sweater. Mrs. Colson was also in a casual pantsuit, in a rust color that complimented her auburn hair. They dined at the Olive Garden and drove down to the nearest shopping mall. It was an outlet center featuring Old Navy, Hush Puppy Shoes, The Dress Barn and other wholesale stores. In the far end was a Cub Foods. Josie wouldn't have to go any further. This mall had it all, including a video store for entertainment. She spent twice the amount of money she had planned; but, it was worth it. She even picked up a Christmas cactus at a home decorating store to place on her kitchen window sill. By the time she gotten her packages home and unpacked, Josie was all in. She fell into bed and slept the sleep of the ecstatically content.

On Sunday, the Colsons took Josie to church with them and out to dinner at Applebees. Josie was feeling a little guilty, like she was imposing on them, intruding on their family outing. However, they treated her like one of the family. Getting to know Mr. Colson, Peter (17) and the twins – Patty and Pauline (13), was a riot. They cracked jokes, teased each other and Josie until they wore down her resistance. They talked about their older brother, Paul, Jr., so much, Josie began to feel as if she knew him, too. P.J., as they called him, was away at graduate school for electrical engineering. She wouldn't get to meet him in person until Easter vacation. After the excitement over the noon meal, and Josie was back at the apartment, she took a much-needed nap. She curled up on the couch with the quilt she had brought from home. Dusk descended on the Big Apple; and, Josie found herself looking forward to the next morning when her new job would officially begin.

Chapter Ten
Getting Started

✟

"Good morning, Josie," Mr. Garvey greeted her when she came into the office with Mrs. Colson. "Did you have a good weekend?"

"Yes, sir! The Colsons are a very friendly and fun-loving family. I am ready to get started," Josie answered. She slid out of her coat and followed Mrs. Colson to the employee break room to hang it up. They placed their lunch bags in the refrigerator before returning to the work area.

"Come with me," Mrs. Colson said. "I will show you where your desk is." She led Josie down the hall three cubicles and over five. This room was a huge grid of desks and dividers where Josie felt she could get lost without much effort. Suddenly, Mrs. Colson stopped, pointing to an empty chair in front of a relatively new computer and company-related text books. Josie set her briefcase under the desk and took a seat. Mrs. Colson demonstrated the use of the telephone and had Josie boot up the computer so she could show her the programs she would be working with.

"These forms are legal documents, so accuracy is a must," Mrs. Colson was saying. "If you make a mistake, try to correct it before printing. If you catch one while proofing the printed document, you must go back into your program to correct it and reprint it on a new form. Some are contracts, others are letters to clients. Either way, the company appreciates perfection. When you are finished with transcribing the information on this tape and have proofed your documents, you may turn them in to Mr. Fredericks, down on the end. He will be your morning supervisor. Any questions?"

"How many documents are there usually on one tape; and, what if I don't get through them all by noon?" Josie asked. "It's been a while since I've done any typing other than my E-mail epistles on the Internet."

"There are usually 8 to 12 documents on each tape. If you do not finish by the time the lunch bell buzzes, simply stop the tape where you are at, make a note on this sticky pad and stick it to the computer screen for Miss Omtvedt. Leave the computer and set where you leave off. She will pick it up form there. Mrs. Peterson is on a time-share job with Miss Omtvedt. So, you will not be able to leave your personal belongings here the entire day."

With that, Mrs. Colson returned to her own desk, leaving Josie to familiarize herself with her new tasks. Josie slipped the headset onto her head and pushed the play button on the tape player. She fished around under the desk for the speed control pedal and found a comfortable setting before typing. After the first couple of forms, she finally had the hang of it; and before she knew it, it was noon. Leaving the computer notated as Mrs. Colson had instructed her, Josie collected her briefcase and headed back down the corridor to the break room. It was bursting at the seams with bustling, chatty coworkers. Each in turn gave Josie a warm smile.

"Welcome aboard," several said.

"Can I get you some coffee?" another asked.

"I hope you enjoy your time here," yet another added.

"Thank you," Josie said to each and every one as she pulled her sack lunch out of the refrigerator. She found a worn brown recliner in the corner where she was able to devour her honey ham-on-cracked wheat along with the pear she had packed. It was amusing to be the mouse in the corner with so many people of both genders devouring their homemade lunches and sharing weekend excursions with each other. This was so different than the mode of operations practiced by the small female crew at Sanderson & Sons. Back there, everyone went their own way, partially because they all had to take turns minding the store; and, partially, because petty jealousy excluded becoming buddies with any one staff member. All too soon, the back-to-work buzzer sounded the end of lunch break. Josie packed her pear core into the plastic sandwich bag and stuffed them both into the brown paper sack, which she promptly deposited in the trash can on her way out the door.

Briefcase in hand, Josie entered Mr. Garvey's office on his heels.

"Come in, come in!" Mr. Garvey said enthusiastically. This man never seemed to frown, Josie noted. "I'd say have a seat; but, we won't be staying here. Today is the monthly managers' meeting in the conference room, down three floors. Did you pack plenty of note paper?"

Josie nodded and patted her briefcase.

"Great! Let's catch an elevator; and, we're on our way." Mr. Garvey grabbed his own briefcase from beside his desk and escorted her down the hall. On the way, he introduced her to Mr. Tuttle who happened to catch the same elevator. The gray haired old man looked a little haggard. He smiled weakly and shook Josie's hand like a limp fish. His slight frame drowned in the chocolate brown suit he had hastily thrown on that morning.

"May I?" Josie asked tentatively reaching for Mr. Tuttle's necktie. When he gave her a brief nod, she straightened it for him. He rewarded her with a bittersweet smile.

"My wife, God rest her soul, used to do that for me every morning," Mr. Tuttle stated. "Maybe, now, the other managers will think I've taken a lover."

Josie chuckled at the attempt at humor then extended her condolences on the loss of his wife.

"She's been gone five years," Mr. Tuttle said. "I still miss her."

The elevator doors opened just then and prevented Josie from asking how his wife died. That was just as well. She didn't want to appear too nosy on her first day. She hoped it was a good sign; though, that he was open with her about such a sensitive subject. She followed the two senior officers into another large room. A 15 foot oval mahogany table took center stage. Several suited people had already selected seats around it. Mr. Garvey went the length of the room to sit at the head of the table. Josie followed Mr. Tuttle and found a chair along the wall behind his seat, halfway down the conference table. She slid a thick notebook, which she had purchased during Saturday's excursion, out of her briefcase along with a three-colored pen and a highlighter. She set her briefcase under her chair to keep it out from under foot and proceeded to head a fresh page with today's date and the heading: *Monthly Manager's Meeting, chair: Mr. Garvey.*

Mrs. Colson entered the room with a trolley cart filled with various forms; hand-outs from each department and the meeting agenda. Mr. Garvey nodded at her; and, she began to distribute the material. After those seated at the table each had one, the excess copies were passed back to those on the side-lines.

I'm going to have to ask Mrs. Colson for a huge three-ring binder to store these in, Josie thought to herself. She noted thankfully the pages were already punched for such storage. She didn't want to think how long it would take her to do it manually.

Once every one had their copies and the paper shuffling had died down, Mr. Garvey opened the meeting and asked for the minutes of last month's meeting. Josie was not surprised to see Mr. Garvey followed Parliamentary Procedures. She wrote down the name of each speaker and their titles at the head of the notes she took on the presentations. On the surface, it was comprehensible. In detail; however, there were several yellow highlighted segments with question marks in her notebook by the end of the three hour session.

Josie was certain Mr. Garvey and Mr. Sloan ran a tight ship. Wherever there were discrepancies or negative numbers where there should be positive ones, Mr. Garvey was on top of it, asking questions, digging into the causes and cures. In one case where the department manager hadn't done his homework, Mr. Garvey suggested he have his answers by the end of the week. There would not be any tabling of the matter until the next meeting. The company couldn't afford another month with those sketchy figures. He wasn't mean, argumentative or aggressive about it; but, the employee got the message loud and clear. His next report would include explanations and answers.

In Mr. Sloan's absence, his executive assistant presented his report. Sloan was in Santa Barbara, California opening a new branch office. He had found a suitable site and bought the land with a habitable building already on it. A reputable cleaning crew had thoroughly scoured the place; and, the furniture and fixtures would be arriving Wednesday. In the meantime, Mr. Sloan was meeting with several employee candidates at the Hilton Hotel, not far from the new office site. Their plans were proceeding ahead of schedule and within budget.

At the good news, a cheer went up from everyone around the table. This expansion was a sure sign of growth in the company. Garvey, Sloan and Associates were now nationwide. They would find a suitable Midwest site, perhaps Chicago or Minneapolis, in five years. In ten, they would cross the border into Quebec and claim international status. Mr. Garvey showed a map on an overhead projector, pointing out the locations of current and prospective company offices. When the lights went up again, he turned to look at Josie.

"Ladies and gentlemen," Garvey said, continuing to gaze at Josie. She began to shake her head side to side, her eyes wide with apprehension. Mr. Garvey just smiled, raised one eyebrow and continued his announcement. "Allow me to introduce our newest employee, Miss Josephine Buchannon. Please stand, Josie. Miss Buchannon will be filling in for Mrs. Peterson who is on maternity leave. It will give her a chance to get acquainted with our *little* company. In her spare time, she will be training with Mr. Tuttle and myself, and, eventually taking over for Mr. Tuttle upon his retirement in May. Please give her a Garvey, Sloan and Associates welcome."

All eyes were on Josie as she withstood the applause that erupted around the room. She gave a slight bow and sat down again. She shot a playful glare in Mr. Garvey's direction.

"That's not all," Mr. Garvey stated as the clapping died away. "I have asked the talented Miss Buchannon to put her advertising skills into developing a new campaign to promote our company. Miss Buchannon comes to us from a reputable advertising firm where her talents garnered her "Top Producer" acclaim for her whole company."

More cheers, clapping and whistles exploded while Josie felt the red blush of embarrassment creep up her neck and face.

"What she doesn't know; however," the CEO continued, "is that she will be one of the lucky few from this office to attend the grand opening of our West Coast branch. I feel it will give her inspiration for her project."

Chapter Eleven
Cinderella Trip

The next six weeks went by in a flurry of learning. Josie tailed Mr. Turtle, as she affectionately thought of Mr. Tuttle, more than she did Mr. Garvey. That was much to her expectations since this was the position she would be filling in not too many more weeks.

Soon, it was the weekend before the Santa Barbara trip; and, Josie was frantically sorting through her wardrobe trying to decide what to pack. It was a bright Saturday afternoon. The March wind had died down for the moment; and, the sun warmed the backyard of the Colson place. Josie dumped her suitcase out for the third time that day and started over. This time, she would start from the bottom, up. One black pair of pumps to go with everything went in followed by one black pair of dressy sandals for evenings on the town, six pair of nude panty hose and three black. Even though she would only be there three days and two nights, it didn't hurt to pack extra. As nervous as she was, she would probably put runs in all of them and then some. Pajamas, bras, bathing suit and toiletries also went into the bottom. The last went into zippered baggies to prevent leakage in case of breakage. Josie carefully folded her three best suits and laid them on top of the undergarments. Navy, black, and fuchsia; she didn't want to be totally conservative. For all she knew, California business women were as colorful as their movie star counterparts. Hmmm, she had better squeeze in the navy pumps as well. Some people would throw a fit if she wore black shoes with a navy suit. A couple of coordinating scarves and a velvet drawstring pouch with her best jewelry; and, she was finished. Finally!

"Now, to pack my briefcase and a small handbag," Josie said to herself. Picking up the travelers checks she had gotten from the area First National Bank, she finished her packing. Just then, there came a knock at the door; and, the Colson twins spilled into the efficient apartment wearing matching royal blue sweat suits and their shoulder length sandy brown hair in ponytails.

"Come outside and play basketball with us!" They chimed.

"Pete's out there hanging up the net right now," Patty said.

"Please help make it a two-on-two," Pauline pleaded. "You can be my teammate!"

"No! I said I get Josie for my teammate!" Patty howled. "No fair!"

Josie hadn't picked up a basketball since she graduated from Lake City Community College nearly two years ago. She said as much; but, that didn't deter the eager young athletes standing before her.

"Okay," Josie said, accepting their invitation. "But, we'll draw straws. The loser gets me!"

They all laughed while Josie grabbed her powder blue down ski jacket from the hook by the door. Leaving the door unlocked, she skipped down the stairs behind the girls. The afternoon passed quickly in the frolicking game where the kids all took turns sharing Josie as their teammate.

Sundays were routine by now. Josie automatically joined the Colsons at church and dinner at some family restaurant. This morning, it was Perkins. Josie ordered a strawberry and whipped cream waffle and a hot chocolate with whipped cream. The twins teased her about being a whipped cream-aholic. Josie laughed and teased them about how they didn't order whipped cream because it would end up on their noses and hide their freckles. Josie tried several times to pay for her own Sunday meals, but Mr. Colson said it was his treat every time. She finally gave up and simply enjoyed the family she never had before.

That night, as Mrs. Colson was kissing the twins good night, the girls were extra bubbly.

"I can't wait until Josie meets P.J.," Pauline said dreamily. "How soon will it be, Easter?"

"Yeah," Patty agreed, hanging over the edge of the top bunk. "Wouldn't it be cool if they fell in love and got married? Then Josie would be our big sister."

"Easter isn't for a couple more weeks," their mother said matter-of-factly. "Besides, you know P.J. has been seeing Pricilla Barnes, that girl he met at college. You met her at Christmas when he brought her home to meet the family."

"Yuck! Prissy Pricilla!" Patty exclaimed, making a sour face. "I thought she was a snob."

"Yeah, I agree," Pauline said. "She was boring, too. She wouldn't play board games with us. I bet she never played basketball in her life!"

"Life is sometimes strange; and, we don't always get what we want. Good night, girls," Mrs. Colson said and shut off the light on her way out of the room.

<*>

Josie awoke before her alarm went off Monday morning. She leapt out of bed and into the shower in record time. Her bags were setting by the door; and, her briefcase and purse were on the small kitchen table. She was too nervous to eat before she left; but, she remembered the company jet would be serving something once they were airborne. Mrs. Colson drove Josie to the airport and personally saw that she and her luggage made it onto the right airplane. It was a good thing Josie had an experienced guide. As nervous as she was, she just might have gotten lost at the airport and missed her flight. Mrs. Colson had come prepared. She handed Josie a little pill case and instructed her to take its contents with water once in the air. It was a sedative and would help her calm down during the coast-to-coast trip. Josie slept the entire flight.

"Are we there already?" she asked in dismay, stifling a yawn. That was some powerful little pill Mrs. Colson had given her. Her stomach growled. That's right, she had missed breakfast. Josie pulled a granola bar out of her briefcase and ate it while she waited for her luggage. She stood around the waiting area with six other Garvey, Loan and Associate employees: Mr. Garvey, of course; Mrs. Sloan, who managed telemarketing, and four vice presidents from various departments. They all piled into the two stretch limousines that waited for them at the curb. The representatives were chauffeured to the Hilton Hotel where they would have a chance to freshen up before a company tour.

The tour lasted nearly two hours. As the East Coast Crew (as they began to call themselves) admired the two-story stucco building with stained glass windows, they began to show signs of jet lag. The seven executives were piled into a hotel shuttle and sent back for a siesta. Even Josie, who had been teased about sleeping the entire flight out, was relieved to be headed back to the hotel. She was also glad she had had the foresight to wear her cushioned walking shoes.

<*>

Josie awoke from a brief nap wondering what she should wear to the banquet that night. Mr. Sloan had arranged a three-meat buffet in honor of the visiting dignitaries and surprised them with the invitation upon their arrival. Would an evening version of her black suit do, or perhaps the sundress she had thrown in at the last second? Opening the closet door, Josie spied an article of clothing hanging there that she hadn't packed. Her hands flew to her face to cover a gasp.

"Oh, my word!" She exclaimed as she drew out a clear plastic-covered evening gown. The sapphire blue sequined formal hung by two delicate chains, presumably straps. The empire waist and darts indicated a snug fit. Twirling the showpiece around, Josie noticed a walking slit in the back, along with an invisible zipper. Flipping back to the front of the frock, Josie saw a tag pinned near the neckline, yet on the outside of the bag. It was a note from someone. Josie hung the dress on the closet door and unpinned the note.

"Dear Josie," she read. "I thought this would come in handy. Be careful not to spill on it – it's rented. Have fun! Love, Darlene."

Josie's heart went out to the executive assistant who had grown into a best friend and mother figure for her over the passed few months. Mrs. Colson had been there for her when no one else had been. With Grams seemingly a thousand miles away, Josie grew to appreciate the friendship as well as the efficiency of the older co-worker.

Walking over to the hotel dresser, Josie pulled her jewelry pouch out of the top drawer. The teardrop sapphire earrings she had brought along to coordinate with her navy suit were a perfect match for the exquisite surprise. The navy pumps, on the other hand, were too businesslike; so, Josie settled for the black strappy heels. After a hot bubble bath and extra time spent on pinning up her hair and coloring an evening face, Josie slipped into the sapphire sequins and the accessories she had set out.

The picture reflected in the full-length mirror was breathtaking. Josie felt lightheaded as she twirled in front of the mirror. Cinderella, that's who she was. And, she had Mrs. Colson to thank for being her fairy godmother. How Darlene ever guessed her dress size, Josie couldn't fathom.

She still had 30 minutes left before she was expected downstairs; so, Josie sat at the desk in her room and brushed clear nail polish on her well-manicured fingernails. It was the finishing touch. Josie sparkled as she emerged from the elevator and embarked on a gala evening of fun, food and new friends.

Still feeling like a movie star at the premier of some new movie, Josie stepped into the stretch limousine waiting for her and her companions at 9:00 the next morning. She shifted her black suit skirt as she sidled across the leather upholstery to make room for Mr. Garvey. The Sloans took the opposite seat, while the other half of their party claimed the limo behind them.

The Grand Opening celebration had been set for 10:00 a.m. Pacific Standard Time with full press coverage. The ribbon would be cut by Sloan and Garvey before they took questions from reporters. A full press package had been sent out the week before; however, the agency partners wanted to give the press their best side along with some personal quotes. These men hadn't risen to the top of their profession without knowing how to schmooze the right people.

Cameras flashed all morning long. Punch and coffee were served along with the traditional mock angel food cake. Josie's face and right hand were beginning to ache from all the smiling and glad-handing she was caught in up. Finally, just when Josie didn't think her legs would hold her up anymore, all the hoopla was over. It was well passed noon; and, she was starved.

"Let's go to lunch," Mr. Garvey proposed as he approached Josie.

"Gladly!" She agreed. They collected the Sloans and made their good-byes to the West Coast executives, new friends she had danced with after the banquet last night. Several eligible bachelors and a couple of not-so-eligible agency men had given Josie their telephone numbers after twirling her around the dance floor. She had received one proposal of marriage and one indecent proposal, both of which she gracefully turned down.

"Where shall we eat?" Mrs. Sloan asked as their limo pulled away from the curb.

"How about the Hard Rock Café?" Josie offered. "I've never been to one; but, I understand there's one in every major city and, they're reported to have the best quarter pound hamburgers in the world." As soon as she had said that, Josie blushed. They must think she's acting like some teenager, eager to go to Pop Tate's malt shop after school.

"That is an excellent idea!" Mr. Garvey exclaimed. "I could go for a burger and fries, myself!"

"Driver, find the nearest Hard Rock Café and step on it!" Mr. Sloan ordered, and gave a decisive nod to his companions. The afternoon passed in pleasant conversation and substantial food.

Later that afternoon, Josie opted to stay in her room and pack rather than join the others in the hotel restaurant for supper. She ordered chicken and wild rice soup and a grilled cheese sandwich via room service and sat back to relax when her chores were completed. She fell asleep watching a rerun of an old comedy on television.

The hotel clerk called Josie's room at 7 a.m. with her wake-up call. The East Coast Crew planned to meet in the lobby at 8 a.m. for a leisurely breakfast before flying home. On the return trip, the passengers kept pretty much to themselves; some slept, others read magazines or newspapers. Josie relived the glamorous vacation in her mind before dropping off to sleep. She dreamed of Hollywood hotels and computer commercials.

Chapter Twelve
Easter Surprise

Once they were all safely back in New York, ensconced in their day-to-day jobs, the East Coast Crew fell into their daily routine and all but forgot about their trip to what Josie liked to think of as "fantasy land". She began to take over more and more of Mr. Tuttle's work. Every other evening she stayed late at the complex so Mr. Tuttle could explain off-season and/or tax reporting activities. Alternating evenings, Josie spent pouring over past advertising promotions and becoming familiar with the work put out by Garvey, Sloan and Associates, LTD (GS&A).

"I don't want to make the fatal mistake of duplicating something that's already been done," she told Mr. Garvey at the onset. The CEO gave her full access to the business complex and put the company archives and screening room at her disposal. Josie was overwhelmed at first. GS&A property and equipment dwarfed and antiquated anything she had ever worked with before. Her saving grace was the kindness and cooperation she encountered in every GL&A employee. Even the projectionist patiently taught Josie how to run the equipment and index whatever data she wanted to view. Within two weeks, she was researching the needed information on her own.

Not even security was a problem GS&A employed only highly bonded staff on all three shifts, and had up-to-the-minute security cameras and motion detectors in every inch of the building and the parking lot. No small-town wannabe killer could get at her here. She was safer here than in her apartment, Josie realized.

Occupied with the added workload, Josie was taken unaware by Easter weekend. She was told the building would be locked up. Only security personnel came in on holidays. She was expected to stay away. So, Thursday evening, Josie called her grandmother to invite her to spend Easter weekend with her in the Big Apple. Josie would sleep on the couch Friday and Saturday evening, offering the comfort of a regular bed to her grandmother.

"And, Grams," Josie added. "We're both invited to Easter dinner at the Colsons'. You'll finally get to meet my landlord and her family."

"That's terrific, Josie," Grams said. "You've told me so much about them when you've called. I feel like I already know them."

With the weekend plans set, Josie said goodbye, locked the door and went to bed.

Sometime after midnight, she was startled awake by a mysterious rattling. Josie sat up in bed and listened in the dark.

There it was again! It sounded like a tugging on a chain. Then it stopped.

"Psst. Pete … are you in there?" A masculine voice called. Someone was trying to get in the door! "Pauline … Patty? Who's in there? Come on! It's P.J. Let me in!"

Josie heaved a sigh of relief. She had been holding her breath, thoughts of her hometown assailant haunting her. She jumped out of bed, wrapped her terry cloth bathrobe around her flannel nightgown and ran down the hall. She stubbed her toe on the end of the couch and had to limp the rest of the way to the door.

"Ouch!" She cried. "Hang on. P.J.! I'm coming."

Josie snapped on the kitchen light before she unchained the door. An astonished P.J. Colson stood on the landing with bugged-out eyes and his mouth hanging open. Josie set a stance with one hand on the door knob and the other on her hip as she looked the intruder up and down. That was P.J., alright. That sandy blonde hair, the Colson blue eyes and those freckles dotting his nose. Not to mention the twins had shown Josie his graduation pictures a few hundred times lately. She stepped aside and motioned him inside. It was drafty standing there with the door open.

"Come in already," she insisted. "It's chilly on the bare feet."

P.J. hefted his duffel bag and crossed the threshold. Once inside, he dropped it onto the couch.

"What the …? Who the …?" P. J. stammered, turning in her direction. He scratched his head and grimaced. "I take it you hadn't heard your folks rented out this apartment," Josie supplied. "Although, I find it difficult to believe that your efficient mother didn't send word. I've been here since the middle of February."

P. J. shook his head and let his brown bomber jacket slide down his arms, catching on his curled fingers.

"She probably tried," he conceded. "I've been out in the field, on-the-job training, since Valentine's Day. I came straight here from there. Actually, I should've been gone before that even, except …" P. J.' s glance dropped to his feet where he bashfully swept the floor with the steel toe of his right boot.

"Except you wanted to spend Valentine's Day with Priscilla," Josie finished for him. P. J.' s head snapped up. He fixed her with a disbelieving glare.

"How did you know?" P.J. asked. "Who ARE you, anyway?"

Suddenly realizing she was alone in her apartment with a strange man, wearing nothing but her nightgown and bathrobe, Josie cringed ever so slightly.

"My name is Josephine Buchannon. My friends call me Josie," she answered. "I am the new Accounts Payable Manager at Garvey, Sloan and Associates where I met your mother. She offered me a better place to stay than the YWCA. Since then, your family sort of adopted me. They talk about you a lot; and, I've seen your picture."

"Adopted you, huh? What are you, some kind of orphan from the country?" the young man asked, finally hanging up his jacket on the peg next to hers.

"In a manner of speaking, yes," Josie replied softly. "My grandmother raised me after my mother died in childbirth. I grew up in Lake City."

"That explains it. Lake City's in the boondocks compared to New York City," P.J. said. "But, what about your father?" Josie slumped into the recliner before answering. P.J. Perched on the arm of the couch with his arms crossed.

"Grams told me my father had gone into the military shortly after he and my mother had ... been together. She said he died in a border skirmish."

She was getting sleepy. In spite of the stimulating conversation, she yawned broadly.

"I'm really sorry," P.J. said, his good upbringing showing through. He stood. "I shouldn't be giving you the third degree in the middle of the night. I just didn't want to wake my family by going into the main house. Mom would've made a fuss. And, I didn't feel like facing them, since Priscilla and I broke up. I didn't feel like talking about it; so, I thought I'd sneak in here instead. This used to be my room you know. I just didn't know you were here."

"Well, I'm not changing the sheets at this hour of the morning," Josie said, standing as well, "but, you're welcome to the bed if you want it. I'll take the couch. That way, you still won't disturb your family."

"No can do. You pay rent – you keep the bed," P.J. insisted. "I'll sleep on the couch." He plopped onto the couch to prove his point. Josie was too tired to argue further; so, she threw him the afghan from the recliner and shuffled off to bed.

Once again, Josie awoke before her alarm went off. She padded to the kitchen to start the coffee and the instant banana bread she had stocked. She paused at the head of the couch to admire the young man, lost in slumber, reclining there. His face reflected innocent repose, his bare chest gleaming in the morning light. P.J. rolled over onto his side and curled into a fetal position. Startled slightly, Josie continued on her way to the stove.

Later, as she was drying off from her shower, Josie heard the oven timer go off. It was snapped off before she could throw on her bathrobe, indicating P.J. had awakened and taken care of it. Hastily, she fixed her face and blew dry her hair. By the time she stepped back into the living area, the table had been set; and, P.J. was sipping a cup of coffee as he waited for her.

"Good morning," she said for lack of anything better.

"Good morning to you, too," he countered. "Say, you clean up pretty good!"

"Thanks, I think," she said, taking a seat opposite him. He cut the banana bread and buttered two slices, one for each of them. Picking up the orange juice carton in one hand and the coffee pot in the other, he lifted one and then the other with a question mark on his face. Josie pointed to the O.J. and he poured.

"Not a coffee drinker?" He asked. "Don't tell me you made coffee just for me?"

"It is the polite thing to do for company," she said. Glancing at the clock, she added, "If you hurry, you can still get ready and go to church with the family. There's Good Friday service, you know."

"Mmm hmm," P.J. tried to talk with his mouth full. He swallowed hard. "That's right! I nearly forgot what day it is. If I catch them just right, maybe they haven't noticed my car in the driveway, yet. They'll think I just arrived."

"Or, been out for a walk," Josie suggested.

"Thanks!" P.J. said, then took one last swig of his coffee. He jumped up, grabbed his jacket and flew out the door.

"You forgot … your duffel bag," Josie finished lamely, not catching him.

By the time Josie made it over to the main house, P.J. had made whatever greetings he had made up his mind to give and went upstairs to shower. Josie joined Mr. and Mrs. Colson in the kitchen while they finished their coffee and waited for the children to brush their teeth and finish dressing.

"P.J. made it home!" Mrs. Colson informed Josie. "I'm glad you're finally going to get to meet him."

"I know," she said. "Actually, I met him at 1 o'clock this morning. I'm sure he didn't tell you; but, he was OJT and didn't get your messages. So, he slept on the couch in the apartment last night. He didn't want to wake you."

"That scalawag!" Mr. Colson exclaimed.

"I'm so sorry!" Mrs. Colson apologized. "He should've been more considerate."

"It was nothing," Josie insisted. "And, he was trying to be considerate – of you!"

"Let's pull a fast one on him," Mr. Colson suggested, conspiratorially. "When he comes down, we'll make the polite introductions. Why don't you go put yours arms around him and give him a big hug and maybe a kiss? You could say something like, 'Didn't you tell your folks where you spent the night?' It'll be a hoot."

Mr. Colson was grinning from ear-to-ear; his eyebrows had disappeared into his hair line. Mrs. Colson was rolling her eyes; but Josie could see she was hiding a smirk. Knowing the family often pulled pranks on each other, she just nodded.

Just then, the object of their plan walked through the kitchen door, dressed remarkably well in a navy sport coat, white shirt (open at the neck) and tan dress pants.

"There he is now," Mr. Colson said. "Josie, I'd like you to meet our oldest child, and my namesake, Paul Jr." He turned back to Josie and winked. Mrs. Colson stood up to clear the coffee cups and hide her face. "Son, this is Josie Buchannon," Paul Sr. continued. "Your mother and I rented the loft above the garage to her."

"How do you do?" P.J. said and held out his hand for her to shake. She ignored it and followed Mr. Colson's previous directions. She slid into P.J.'s arms and planted a romantic kiss on his lips. At first, it seemed as if he was beginning to respond in kind. His arms pulled in around her waist and his lips hinted a welcome. Suddenly, he remembered his parents were watching; and, he pulled back.

"What's going on here?" P.J. demanded.

"What's the matter, P.J.? Didn't you tell your parents where you spent the night, last night? Didn't you tell them you sneaked into my bed?" Josie purred like some TV starlet she had seen in a romantic movie. "Of course, you didn't realize I'd be there, but you warmed up to the idea quickly enough."

Before she had quite finished P.J. had dropped his hand and stepped back. Josie also fell back and dropped into the chair she had been sitting in before his entrance. Mrs. Colson turned around and put her hands on her husband's shoulders.

"Gotcha!" The three perpetrators chorused. They all had a good laugh, then P.J. came clean about sleeping on the couch. He was in the middle of telling his parents about breaking up with Priscilla when his siblings marched into the room.

"You broke up with Prissy Priscilla?" Patti shouted. "Hurray!"

"She was such a snob! I didn't like her," Pauline declared.

Pete clapped his brother on the back and stuck an approving thumb in the air.

"What happened, anyway, son?" His father asked.

P.J. looked around at his family, then at Josie. Well, he had to say it sooner or later. He might as well get it over with.

"I gave her two tickets to the Country Jamboree campout in June as a Valentine gift. Reba McIntyre is a headliner!" He said defensively. "She threw the tickets back in my face like they were dirt. I asked her if she was expecting something else, like maybe a diamond ring; and, she said yes. I asked her to come home with me Easter weekend; maybe the Easter Bunny would give her one in one of those plastic eggs. She screamed we were through and stomped of. I went off on OJT and worked hard to forget about her."

Everyone laughed. Leave it to a Colson to get shot down because of his sense of humor. Josie felt sorry for him. It was obvious they shared the same appreciation for Country Music. She wouldn't have thrown the tickets in his face, she realized. She would even appreciate the sentiment of finding a diamond ring instead of candy in an Easter egg.

"You're better off without her, P.J.," Mrs. Colson said, "especially, if she can't appreciate your warm sense of humor."

The Colson's and Josie squeezed into their minivan and just barely made it to church on time. Josie lagged behind at the doorway, hoping she would get to sit by P.J. Her wish came true, but made it terribly difficult for her to concentrate on the sermon.

Later that day, Josie's grandmother arrived right on the dot of 5 o'clock. Josie helped her carry the myriad of boxes and suitcases up to the apartment. Most of it was Josie's spring and summer wardrobe. She tore into each box searching for last year's Easter outfit. The white floral sundress and lavender jacket would seem new to the Colsons. Later, she and Grams popped some popcorn and watched the Resurrection Story on television.

On Saturday, Josie took her grandmother on the same tour Mrs. Colson had taken her on her first weekend in the Big Apple. As they passed a jewelry store on the mall, Josie noticed a couple at the counter inside. The woman was admiring a large engagement ring by holding her hand in the air. Her prospective spouse stood behind her protectively. Thinking about how important diamonds still were in these modern times, an inkling of a company ad began to take shape in Josie's mind. She shook her head and moved on.

Josie took Grams to the Olive Garden for lunch. Why not show her the exact same trip Mrs. Colson showed her, Josie thought. Over pasta and dinner rolls, Josie asked her grandmother to catch her up on what was happening in Lake City.

"You'll want to know everything about Sanderson & Sons," Grams guessed. "Do you remember those company ads you were working on just before you left? I've seen them both. The one on TV turned out great, Josie Girl! The paper ad you planned for magazine coverage ended up on a billboard at the edge of town – with Cass' by-line."

"I told you, Grams," Josie said and leaned in to whisper to her companion. "I told you that woman stole my ideas. So, what else have you heard or seen?"

"Well, Sanderson & Sons is sporting a new sign out front," Eleanor continued. "I don't recall seeing any of your ideas for that, but I remember you saying you suggested it. It shows some space-age scenery and promises 22nd century service at 20th century prices."

"That's a bad take on the concept I was trying to promote," Josie said, nearly choking on her roll as she laughed.

"You're right; it does look pretty cheesy," Grams agreed, and laughed with her.

That evening, while Eleanor showered, Josie took out her story boards and began tracing out the logo she had in mind for GS&A. Her aqua charcoal pencil received a good workout as she sketched the company building in the background. In the foreground, she drew a couple on a park bench. He was on bended knee having just proposed. They were admiring the rock on her hand. The statement read: A diamond is forever, just like the rock solid advertising service provided by Garvey, Sloan and Associates, LTD, New York and Santa Barbara, 1-800-WIN-WINS. Dreamily, Josie penciled directions for a photo shoot. Ask P.J. Colson to play the part of the man in the ad. She racked her brain to think of a GS&A employee to fill the other role. She finally remembered that the executive assistant to Mr. Sloan looked somewhat like herself. So, she jotted down her name – Amelia Henderson, Ami for short. After a few other notes to make the scene animated for television, she pushed it aside and started a kettle for hot chocolate and chamomile tea.

Josie and her grandmother attended church with the Colsons Easter morning, driving separately. They sat behind the Colsons and joined them again at home for a very pleasant turkey dinner with all the trimmings.

"Thank you so much," Josie told Darlene as she and Grams were leaving the house mid-afternoon. "You and your family have made this one of the best holidays I've even had!"

Mrs. Colson gave her a hug and a kiss on the cheek.

"You are welcome, dear. You may pop over anytime you feel like company, you know," Darlene told her. "Everyone here thinks of you as part of the family. And, I'm so glad your grandmother could join us." She reached out to shake the older lady's hand and bid her good-bye.

Josie walked her grandmother to her car and wished her a safe trip home.

"This move to New York seems to be turning out all right," Josie told her grandmother. "I really like the Colsons and my job. Your coming for Easter was the icing on the cake."

"God lets bad things happen to good people for reasons we can't always see right away," Grams said, paraphrasing a Bible passage. Josie realized Grams was referring to the way she had been forced out of her old job versus the benefits of her new position at Garvey, Sloan and Associates, LTD. However, it could also apply to the home and family department, and the prospect of a developing romance.

"You give me a call when you get home, Grams. Then, I'll know you made it back safely," Josie said as she kissed her grandmother on the cheek. "Call me, too, if you hear of anything else going down at Sanderson & Sons that I should know about."

"I will, dear," her grandmother said as she returned the kiss Josie had given her. Then she headed north to Lake City and home.

Chapter Thirteen
Inheritance

Josie had rushed back into the Colson house after seeing her grandmother off. She didn't want to lose a precious second of spending time with P.J. Colson.

While she was playing charades with the Colson family, her ex-boss was playing a different kind of game. Cass had offered to make Easter dinner for Lew at his house in Deer Valley and intended to serve him his Last Supper. Before arriving at his house around 1 p.m., she had spent the morning driving into New York City to check into a hotel for the night. She had packed a gray beret to wear with her only gray suit. She changed into them, tucking all her hair into the floppy headpiece and returned to the registration desk.

"Can you make a few suggestions where to dine tonight if I were looking for something more exotic than what is on the menu in your restaurant?" She asked the concierge, slipping him a $20 bill. With written directions in hand, she drove away – back to Lew's, picking up a take-out dinner from an unknown deli on the way back This would be a day to remember, Cass thought as she fished in her leather handbag for a little brown prescription bottle. She had told Lew she would park around back so she could bring the dinner in the back door. What she really wanted was for no one to know she had been there. Hopefully, everyone would be out-of-town or too busy to look out the window when she arrived. Just in case, Cass had picked up a rental car the day before. She planned to tell Lew the Lexus was in the shop.

"Pretty soon it will all be mine!" Cass said to herself as she caressed the pill container.

The telephone on Josie's desk jangled her out of a near-trance. She had been working so hard on the monthly payroll; she jumped a foot out of her chair.

"Accounts Payable; this is Miss Buchannon. Can I help you?" Josie recited. She grabbed her note pad and poised a pen.

"Josephine Buchannon, originally from Lake City?" A masculine voice asked. Josie answered in the affirmative. "This is Sidney Silverstein, attorney for the late Llewellyn Sanderson.

"Hello, Mr. Silverstein. I recognize your name," Josie said. "Did I hear you correctly? Did you say the 'late' Lew Sanderson?"

"Yes, I'm afraid I am the bearer of bad news. Well, in your case, it could be good news, depending on your perspective," Silverstein said cryptically. "Mr. Sanderson mentioned you in his will. So, I'm calling to set an appointment with you to discuss the bequest. Are you free for lunch any day this week? I could pick up some sandwiches or something and bring them along."

"Thursday and Friday are both available," Josie offered. "But I could order something from the deli across the street. We could either eat there or have it delivered."

"Thursday, it is, then. Have it delivered, if you like," Silverstein agreed. "If you can get a private conference room, it would be preferable. I don't think you want this going public just yet. Order me a turkey-and-cheese on rye with mustard and coffee."

"I can set that all up for you," Josie said. "Just one thing before you hang up: How did it happen?"

"Between you, me and the fence post, the police think it was murder," Silverstein answered. "By the way, call me 'Sid'. I think we'll be spending a lot of time together. See you Thursday at noon."

Sid never told Josie what he looked like, but it wasn't hard to figure out he was the short, balding man in the tan suit and matching fedora that found his way to her office at 12 sharp two days later. After the perfunctory handshaking and introductions, Josie led Sid down the hall to her floor's conference room. Schlotzky's Deli had already delivered their lunches and set a fine picnic table. While Josie poured coffee for Sid and water for herself, Sid opened his briefcase and pulled out important looking documents. Duplicate copies were laid out so each of them could read from his or her own.

Between mouthfuls of his cold sandwich, Sid revealed a shocking, long-kept secret that nearly knocked Josie right out of her chair.

"Twenty years ago, when Lew first put me on retainer, he made me swear an oath to him," Sid began. "He told me about this lovely young artist who was going to be his bride when he returned from military service. His patrol party got lost in a boarder skirmish along enemy lines. He was missing in action for nearly a year. When he returned, he heard of the shocking demise of his beloved fiancée. They had never told anyone about their engagement; and apparently, the young woman never breathed his name after he left for his tour of duty. She died giving birth to a healthy baby girl who was raised by her maternal grandmother."

Josie nearly choked on her tuna salad sandwich. Sid paused seeing how wide Josie's eyes had become as it dawned on her she was the baby of whom he was speaking.

"The oath I swore to, as Lew's attorney, was to find his daughter when he died and make sure she inherited everything he had to offer," Sid continued. "Fortunately, I didn't have to look far."

"B-but … why … does Grams know?" Josie stuttered. "You mean Sanderson & Sons is … *mine?*"

"Oh, much more than just Sanderson & Sons," Sid said empathetically. "Your biological father was worth $4.5 million dollars in cash and properties – and, that is after your inheritance taxes. Why didn't he ever tell you? When he first returned, he was single and had a business to build. He didn't have the time, energy or nurturing skills to take on an infant. He knew you were better off with your grandparents. No, your grandmother doesn't know. I had to tell her Lew left you 'a little something' in order to get your whereabouts out of her. She wasn't aware just how close Lew and your mother had been. She thinks all the employees at the ad agency are getting 'a little something'."

"But, $4.5 million? What am I going to do with all that?" Josie wondered out loud. "You said properties. Did he own more than the agency?"

"Oh, yes, Josie. Lew owned half the business district in Lake City. Most of it is either empty lots or empty buildings, but it still has a good market value," Sid said. "Here, take a look at this map. You can see this shaded area here, going to the west of the ad agency; and, that movie theater that nearly closed last year. There are other lots here, here and here. They total about $2 million; the rest is in long and short –term stocks, bonds and treasury notes, most of which are due to come due next month. And, of course there's family residence in Deer Valley."

"Speaking of family," Josie said, "what about his sons? Wouldn't they get a cut?"

"Lew never actually had any other children," Sid explained. "He named the business Sanderson & Sons in the event he would eventually have some, but he never married. Even if he had, as his first-born and following in his footsteps, as it were – having actually worked at the agency, you would still stand to inherit at least the business."

"My word! I'm an heiress!" Josie exclaimed. "Can I have a few days to take this all in? I'm speechless!"

"By all means, take your time," Sid advised. "With this kind of inheritance comes a great deal of responsibility. You wouldn't want to fritter it away, make bad investments or flaunt it; especially, with a murderer on the loose."

"That's right!" Josie said. "Do the police have any clues, any suspects?"

"Yes, they do, but they're keeping it under tight wraps for now," Sid said. "The agency personnel aren't talking, claiming to be too shook up. They all seem to have alibis for Easter Sunday when it happened. Reports claim he was drugged. Other than that, who knew? The authorities want to work closely with you when you take over. They are hoping you will use some of the ready reserve cash to remodel the office and install hidden cameras and recording devices; somehow, without the employees' knowledge. So, while you are contemplating your next move, keep that in mind. In fact, it should be your top priority. I have not yet announced who the heir is. I think the transition should be done as quickly and as quietly as possible. I have to tell you, Josie, Cassandra Coven has been hounding my office for a public reading of the will. I get the feeling she thinks she inherited Sanderson & Sons."

"There are office rumors she and Lew were having an affair," Josie said, nodding. "I try never to pay attention to rumors – unless they involve me. If those rumors were true, I can see where Cass would assume she was named in the will, but isn't it rather presumptuous to think she would get the agency?"

"First, the rumors were true. Lew never kept secrets from me; we were best friends," Sid said. "And, secondly, they were together nearly four years. The way things were going, it could have made it to the common law marriage requirement – had they actually been living together. I advised Lew to keep separate dwellings for this very reason. So, no; it wouldn't be out of line for Miss Coven to expect something. It's time for me to leave. Here is your copy of the will. I want to come back Monday or Tuesday and go over your thoughts. I don't trust the telephone lines to discuss something this big."

Josie paid her condolences to Sid on the loss of his friend and escorted him back to the elevator. Not wanting to put it off another day, Josie scheduled the conference room for 11 a.m. Monday, Any later, and they would run into the weekly staff meeting.

Over the weekend, she couldn't think of anything else. She didn't even realize P.J. had been home. She was wrapped up in thought and pen and paper, hibernating in her apartment, while P.J. was busy filming the agency ad for GS&A. Their paths never crossed; although, P.J. left a note attached to a single long-stemmed pink rose for her at the main house. She would have received it when she went to church with the family. P.J. had already returned to his OJT. The twins delivered it to her.

"I missed you this weekend. Hope to spend time with you next trip. – P.J." the note read.

Chapter Fourteen
The Princess Plan

Josie had opted to skip church that weekend to work on her "Princess Plan", as she called it. So, Pattie and Pauline were her only contact with the Colsons the morning she received the rose from P.J. Considering the delivery persons, Josie didn't put much stock in the fact that it had actually come from the signer. The girls had been plotting and matchmaking all spring. This was just the sort of trick they would pull. Josie plucked a bud vase from the kitchen cupboard to display the rose for the twins' benefit and went back to work.

Before she knew it, Josie was seated across from Sid in the accounting department's conference room once again. This time she was better prepared. She had with her a spiral notebook with all the notes she had drawn up over the weekend.

"So, what did you come up with?" Sid asked.

"Well, I figured the only way to keep Cass and the others busy so they wouldn't notice the bugs going into the walls was to hire them to develop ads for several new businesses going into Lake City. And, the only way to keep them guessing is to set up new corporations with the ready reserve. That way they can run anonymously. I figure the longer we can keep Cass in the dark about the new owner, the better. I want you to set up a $100,000 trust fund for Cass as a gift from Lew. She won't be happy, but it will throw her off track. Tell her Lew had an illegitimate heir, but you are still trying to locate this person – no gender mentioned. Whatever you do, don't tell her how big the estate is; don't tell anyone! Here's what I want you to do with the main street properties …"

Within two weeks, Sid had hired contractors through dummy corporations to refurbish the empty buildings on Main Street. On the corner, the old Jackson's Meat Market was remodeled to house an employment agency. In the adjoining building, Sid started a youth center. The complex was called the Lake City Community Services building. It would provide food and beverage vending machines, an arcade and telephone services to teens who had to wait for a ride home after sporting events or needed a safe, fun place to hang out on weekends. It would offer a security guard and a juke box, as well.

Two doors down, a vacated Swiss style office building would quickly be restored. It would be christened Lake City Lutheran Services and offer scholarship programs to area Lutheran colleges and office space to visiting Thrivent Insurance agents. With an infusion of funds, the dying movie theater was renovated into a community playhouse. It would house all the amateur musical productions that were once held in the old school building, which Josie had learned was recently condemned. Fine Arts Grants from another of Josie's trust funds provided the needed backing for this project.

Speaking of the old school building, the Lake City Collective School District had been frightfully unsuccessful in its efforts to sell the old site or find practical uses for it, especially now that part of the building had been condemned.

Josie, through Sid and yet another dummy corporation, purchased the old site and hired a wrecking crew to tear down the condemned portion and put up an indoor pool and handicap accessible locker rooms. They would also convert all the newer classrooms into community education rooms and old-fashioned YMCA boarding rooms, once the wiring was brought up to code. This project alone took up most of the ready reserve; however, Sid was a resourceful person and came up with some funding of his own through federal grants and private donations.

Meanwhile, Sid hired spokesmen for some of the new corporations who, in turn, hired Sanderson & Sons to promote the new businesses. Sid represented the remainder and did likewise. At the same time, he hired specialists to remodel the offices of Sanderson & Sons without explaining the details to Cass. Two new offices would be built, one for Cass and one for the new owner – once he or she was found. A new accountant was hired for the agency. Nathan Danielson, a young family man, had just been laid off from the local bank due to down-sizing. Josie thought it would be a good touch to help him avoid moving away to find employment. This way, he could keep his elementary-age children in the school they had become accustomed to. Sid also hired Victoria, aka Vikki, Bresson, Josie's best friend, who had just graduated from the secretarial program at Lake City Community College, to replace Donna Schmidd at the front desk. Donna's skills would be better utilized in the production room, assisting Hildy. Perky Vikki's bubbly personality and blond good looks would better serve at the front desk.

Josie had seriously considered trying to find Sherry Ingram and offer her old job back. However, she had heard through the grapevine that Ingram had found a better job in the Big Apple and was making twice the money as a seamstress at an exclusive dress shop. Besides, if too many of the old faces began popping back into the picture, it would serve as a red flag for Cass.

Sid visited Josie one more time in May. It was the last day of the month and GS&A personnel were gearing up to take inventory. Their fiscal year ended June 30; and, it took a whole month to count everything, even with the dozens of people involved in each department.

"Everything's in place, Josie," Sid reported. "I had to pull a few strings and grease a few palms, but I think you will be pleased with the progress. You have to realize it isn't easy to get qualified professionals on such short notice. I had to hire extra help to write grants and push them through. Some aren't even back yet, because the deadlines were so far away. I am confident; though, that we had good people on every aspect of your plan. Money talks. The other good news is, even though you are low on ready reserve and all your paper securities were cashed in to fund this bomb, almost all of it went into improvements in existing properties creating a huge jump in their net worth. All the legal paperwork should be completed next month. About the time Lake City celebrates Independence Day, you should be able to disclose your identify. We wouldn't want to wait much longer than that or we will run out of advertising jobs for Sanderson & Sons."

"Sounds good, Sid," Josie said, smiling appreciatively. "I can imagine it wasn't easy to manipulate so many different people. Some of them are probably wondering how legal all this is if you're trying to rush it through so fast. In fact, I hope we didn't do anything illegal by setting up those dummy corporations."

"Well, I may have stretched it a little," Sid admitted, scratching the edge of his hairline and squinting. "But, I filled out all the necessary forms, talked to the right people and used the real friends and relatives' names as corporation officers. Everything is double insured and bonded. It should be okay. I had you sign all the proper paperwork and it's all been filed at the county court house. Your name should be buried deep enough that a casual dig on Cass' part shouldn't unearth it."

"Well, that's good," Josie said, and heaved a sigh. "I guess all that's left is to draw up a big advertising splash for the debut. Or, should I leave that in the hands of Sanderson & Sons, too?"

"No, I think it would be better if you did it. You want it done right; and, this will be the perfect opportunity to show that the new owner is capable of running the company," Sid said. After a reflective pause, he added, "Have you given your notice here, yet?"

"Actually, no. I have been working on the letter at home. I just wasn't sure when to date it," Josie said. "Now, I know. I will date it June 1st and give them one month's notice. I'm sure they have a file a mile long of prospective replacements. It shouldn't take them any longer that that. I just hope we're done with my major company promotion by then. I've been so busy with inventory and this project to even check on the progress."

"So, what idea did you run with?" Sid asked.

"That's the kicker; I don't even know," Josie said as she walked Sid to the door. "I submitted three of them and told Mr. Garvey to pick one. He said he and Mr. Sloan had made the decision, but he was rushing out to meet a client and didn't have time to tell me which one. I guess I'll just have to be surprised."

Chapter Fifteen
Homecoming

Josie never did get an opportunity to discuss her ad campaign with anyone. Even Mrs. Colson seemed to have forgotten it or was keeping it a secret. The only clue Josie had had, the rose, she had dismissed out of hand.

With the Princess Plan in the works, every weekend was filled with reviewing reports from Sid, making architectural decisions and planning her coming out party. Through Cass, via Sid, Josie ordered meat and cheese trays, coffee and punch for the open house reception. They also ordered helium balloons for all the desks, streamers and confetti. She wanted this to be a real celebration; and, if it overwhelmed Cass with the thought of cleaning up all that mess, all the better!

Ooh! That's right! The one position Josie had nearly forgotten was that of a cleaning lady. Well, if Sid couldn't find anyone by the date of the reception, perhaps Gram's friends at Club would come in to help on this one occasion. Josie made note to talk to Sid about that.

The remainder of June went by in a flurry. Her last day at GS&A had been a bittersweet one. The office gave her a going away party with cake and balloons. The accounting department had chipped in to buy her a new set of charcoal pencils and story boards. Mr. Garvey and Mr. Sloan presented her with an expensive alligator briefcase. Mr. Garvey and Darlene Colson promised to be at her debut in Lake City in just a couple of weeks. Josie cried until her makeup had washed away; and, then she cried some more on Saturday when the Colsons saw her off. P.J. couldn't make it home, but he had sent her a going away card and promised he would accompany his family to her debut at Sanderson & Sons.

All too soon, Josie was packed up and moved back into the Victorian Drama Style house on Willow Lane in Lake City, upstate. Josie tried to catch her breath. She took the weekend to unpack and set up two appointments at Connie's Cut 'N' Curl, along with a manicure. She felt like it was prom week, having to have a practice session before and the "real thing" on the day of the special event. In this case, the day was Friday. Today was Monday – she now had four days to write her acceptance speech.

That evening, she sat down on Gram's Victorian love seat with notebook in hand. Some of her best work was done in long hand. She would transfer it to a computer printout later. There was a knock at the door, but Eleanor rushed out of the kitchen calling out that she would get it. A moment later, she strode into the living room with a two-part special delivery.

"Wow, Grams! That's some bouquet of flowers," Josie exclaimed. She dropped her work on the loveseat and rushed to smell the brilliantly colored blossoms. There were lilacs, daisies, pink carnations, baby's breath and greenery. Standing in the center was on long-stemmed red rose.

"They're for you," Grams said and handed over the bulky glass vase and its fragrant contents. "There's also a smaller package here. Read the flower card first, then open this."

"Josie tore open the tiny white linen envelope and slid out the dainty card from inside. It was written in the usual floral shop clerk's penmanship, so that was no clue. "Mom said she was sending the video of the GS&A commercial to you, so I thought I would send these flowers with it," she read aloud. "Can't wait to see you Friday. Love, P.J."

"Well, wasn't that sweet," Grams commented. She traded the brown paper package for the bouquet and set the flowers on the desk so Josie could unwrap the video.

"The flowers are gorgeous," Josie demurred. And, they're too expensive for the twins to have sent. *Maybe that rose last month* **was** *from P.J., after all*, Josie thought. Then she unwrapped the video. There was also a short note in there from Darlene about hoping she liked it and sorry Josie hadn't gotten to see it before she had had to leave. "Okay, let's plug in the video."

Before her very eyes, Josie's campaign took life. The camera spanned the breath of the aqua agency headquarters. It gleamed against the May sunshine. Soon it zoomed in on the couple on the park bench near the company parking lot.

"Say, that couple looks familiar," Grams commented, pointing at the screen. "Who is that girl? She looks a lot like you, but I know it's not you. And, that's P.J., isn't it?"

"Yes, Grams. Shhh!" Josie said, not wanting to miss a thing. She watched with bated breath as P.J. slipped a spectacular diamond engagement ring on Ami's finger. Ami, short for Amelia, was now Mr. Sloan's executive assistant. She would explain to Gram's later, but for now, Josie just wanted to lose herself in the scene before her and pretend it was herself sitting there admiring the object of her new commitment with P.J. She could see herself wearing a slinky slip dress and matching sandals instead of the heather gray sweat suit she was now wearing.

"Diamonds are still forever," Dan Bakker's voice rang out. Bakker worked in accounting where Josie had heard that rich baritone voice on a daily basis. "Just like the rock solid advertising services of Garvey, Sloan and Associates, LTD. Offices in New York and Santa Barbara."

As the 800 number flashed on the screen above the couple, Josie reached over to shut off the television.

"It turned out great, Josie Girl," her grandmother said. She patted Josie on the back. "I almost thought that was you getting engaged to P.J. Was that why you picked someone that looked like you? Do you have feelings for him? Or, was that a fluke?"

"No, Grams," Josie admitted. She draped herself over the couch facing her grandmother. "No, it wasn't a fluke. I designed it that way for that very reason. I shouldn't be saying this, but, yes, I think I'm falling in love with P.J. Colson."

Friday morning dawned early, yet Josie was up before the sun. She had practiced her speech until she was blue in the face and finally went to bed around midnight. Today, she slid out of bed and switched on the light. She wanted to set out her new outfit for this afternoon's festivities.

After receiving an invitation for Josie's debut with a note to be discreet, Sherry Ingram had called Josie at GS&A to take her to lunch. She had to pick up the same deli food as Sid Silverstein had gotten; and, considering Josie's schedule, she felt that was fair. She surprised Josie by taking her measurements and providing her with a custom fit designer suit at cost, free silk stockings and a pair of matching pumps at 30% off from a nearby shoe store. Since she had saved up quite a bit of her salary from the larger advertising agency, Josie jumped at the offer.

Holding the navy power suit over her nightgown where she could admire the sequins and scrolling braid on the fitted jacket in the dresser mirror, Josie stood in awe. She remembered how exhilarating it was to try it on the first time. Josie draped the outfit carefully over the foot end of her brass bed and went back to the dresser to fish out the stockings. She had actually gotten two pair, just in case one ran, and laid them both near the suit. She didn't have to go much further for her new Italian pumps. She had left them wrapped snugly in their tissue paper and cradled in the box they had come in, set on top of her bureau.

Then came a luxurious bubble bath, a leisurely breakfast with Grams and the second trip to the hair dresser. Earlier in the week Josie had had her helmet hair style shortened to a bouffant and styled more professionally than she had ever had it done before. Until then, it had seemed sufficient to pull the sides back into a tortoise shell barrette and let it go at that. Connie, the hairdresser, prodded Josie for information on what the special occasion was that she had had to have two hair appointments. Josie answered with a description of the successful ad campaign she had written for GS&A. She told Connie she was treating herself and wanted to be prepared for the big event when her boss celebrated her success. That seemed to satisfy the naturally nosy beautician.

By the time 12 noon had arrived, Josie was too nervous to eat lunch. Grams insisted she drink some chamomile and lavender tea to calm her jangled nerves. Josie took the extra precaution of rubbing lavender lotion on her feet and hands. Its calming influence would stay with her throughout the afternoon.

Josie and Sid had agreed to drive separately to Sanderson & Sons. It would continue the air of mystery; and, it seemed fitting that she attend the doings with her grandmother. So, promptly at 2:10 p.m., the two women walked into the business establishment Josie had fled only six months earlier. Sid had arrived at 1:45 p.m., seemingly to go over the agenda with Cass.

The agency manager was drawn to Josie like a moth to a flame in spite of the wall-to-wall crowd that had appeared. Cass worked her way over to where Josie was helping herself to a piece of marble bakery cake.

"Well, well, well," Cass drawled, parking herself point-blank in Josie's path. She drew herself up on the tips of the department store pumps she had selected to go with the new black suit she had purchased for Lew's funeral. "Look what the wind blew in. So, Josie, where have you been hiding yourself these passed few months? It was certainly a shock to get your resignation the way I did. Just what kind of job was so important it couldn't wait the proper notice period?"

"I took a job with Garvey, Sloan and Associates, LTD, in New York," Josie answered when Cass finally gave her a chance. She had to think on her feet in order to come up with a plausible excuse. "It was spur of the moment because the deadline for the applications had already passed, but they liked my resume so I got a hasty interview. I'm really sorry it went down that way, Cass. You know it isn't like me to leave anything undone."

"Yeah, right," Cass snorted. "By the way, aren't you a little overdressed for this occasion? You'd think you were the guest of honor in that get-up."

She walked away before Josie could reply. Josie watched Cass strut over to a tiny staging area in the back corner of the main room. She must have borrowed a band box from the high school or college band director, because with one step she had risen a foot above the crowd. Sid was by her side and handed her a microphone.

"Testing. Testing one-two," Cass spoke into the mike. "Welcome, everyone! Thank you for coming to our special open house. Most of you know me. I'm Cassandra Coven, the manager here at Sanderson & Sons. With us today is our late owner, Llewellyn Sanderson's attorney. He has promised to end the mystery of Lew's legal heir today. So, without further adieu, I give you Sid Silverstein."

The 80-some attendees standing elbow-to-elbow applauded politely. Exchanging places with Cass, Sid took the microphone from her.

"It was a mournful message to receive on Easter Monday," Sid began, nearly choking on his words. His eyes shot toward the ceiling as his lips pulled down into a grimace. He pulled a white linen handkerchief from his double-breasted navy suit and dabbed his eyes. "Some of you know how close Lew and I were. We weren't just business associates, we were best friends. I hope you will forgive me for saying this, but I hope the authorities catch whoever sent him to his reward before I do, or I may have to find someone to represent me!

"Anyway, the silver lining around this thundercloud is that Lew was aware of an heir to his estate." Sid paused a moment to let that fact sink in. He glanced around the room and spotted Josie who had worked her way closer to the corner where she would have to be shortly. "When he first hired me twenty years ago, he made me swear an oath to keep his secret and to find that heir if anything ever happened to him. He made me swear I would make sure this child of his would receive everything he had built. What a lot of you don't know is just exactly how much he had built. That part of the story will be left for another day. Today, we celebrate with Sanderson & Sons Advertising Agency the return of its rightful owner – Miss Josephine Buchannon!"

At the sound of her name, the crowd parted and allowed Josie to approach Sid and the microphone. A cheer went up and thunderous applause shook the building. Along the way, Josie got a good shot at Cass' face. Just as she had expected, it wore an expression of total shock mixed with evil fury. It was a good thing Sid was there to help her onto the platform, because her knees went weak with fear from the sight. She took a deep breath and steadied herself just as the clapping died down.

"Thank you! Thank you!" Josie acknowledged. She took another deep breath, letting it out slowly as she surveyed the crowd. Many familiar faces were scattered among the strangers. All of them were grinning at her. All but Cass, that is. Thunder clouds were forming over her head and lightening flashed in her slitted green eyes.

"I know I left under mysterious circumstances in January," Josie admitted. She switched the mike to her right hand before continuing. "I'm sure Sid would vouch for me that I had a life-or-death reason for doing so. Suffice it to say, I landed a great job at Garvey, Sloan and Associates, LTD, in New York. In fact, my employer, Mr. Garvey, is here today, as well as his administrative assistant and my dear friend, Mrs. Darlene Colson and her family. Mr. Sloan had planned to be here as well, but I am told he had to fly to Chicago to seal the deal on their second branch office. I guess they will have to edit the company ad I did for them to include the word 'Chicago' under the engaged couple in the picture.

"Yes, that's right. That was my work," Josie said as several people whispered compliments to their neighbors regarding the commercial they had seen on television or in the magazine ad they had seen. Josie didn't dare look at Cass. She would get her reaction from Sid later. "I had a speech written and practiced, but right now, all I can think of to say, is it will be 'business as usual' at Sanderson & Sons. We will continue to give this community our very best efforts. And, now, with the new and improved office building, we should be more efficient than ever."

Chapter Sixteen
Old and New Friends

To the tune of still more applause, Josie handed the microphone back to Sid and let him help her down. She would gladly have stayed up there to hide behind his back as he dismissed the open house crowd, but there was just enough room up there for one person. She kept telling herself the announcement had been a huge success and Cass wouldn't try anything stupid with all these witnesses present.

Suddenly, flashbulbs were exploding in Josie's eyes as the newspaper photographers did their jobs. There had been a few shots taken while she was at the mike, but they seemed to come out of the woodwork, now.

"Can we get a shot of you and Ms. Coven shaking hands?" One of them asked. Josie was shoved toward Cass. She blindly reached out her hand in Cass' direction. Cass clasped her hand in a gruff manner and gave a practiced smile for the press. The rest of the afternoon, Josie spent receiving congratulatory hugs and handshakes. Even the mayor was on hand to welcome Josie back to town and into the business community. By the time the last guest had left, Josie's feet were ready to call in the fire department. They were hot and achy, not having been used to high heels.

Josie sank into the nearest folding chair and slipped off her new pumps. Grams glided over and took a seat next to her. Sid wasn't far behind. Josie had warned him not to leave the room while she was still there. She didn't want to be caught alone with Cass.

"Well, Pussycat, you did good," Grams said in her country vocabulary. She, too, kicked off her lilac pumps and wiggled her stockinged toes. "It's a darn good thing it's Saturday tomorrow. We can both sleep in. I think we deserve it after today."

"We can't sleep in too late, Grams," Josie said. She wagged her index finger at Eleanor. "Remember, we planned to come down here with your Club friends to clean up after this shindig."

"That won't be necessary," Sid interjected as he pulled his chair close to Josie. "I managed to get hold of the Always Better and Cheaper crew. The ABCs have a great reputation. They are hometown ladies who really know their stuff. I told them I would meet them here at 8:00 tomorrow morning and let them in."

Cass had strolled over to their little huddle in time to catch everything Sid had just said. She leaned a hand on the back of his chair and fixed the little group with a disdainful glare.

"Well! Thank God you aren't leaving this mess for me to clean up! I was beginning to wonder if I would get paid overtime for it – because it sure as heck would have taken me all weekend to do it," Cass complained.

Feeling a confidence she had never felt before, Josie looked Cass in the eye. She stood up and went nose-to-nose with her new subordinate.

"Look here, Cass. You have been given a raise, a new office, a new computer and an extra floating holiday. I would think a little appreciation is in order," Josie stated. Then she did something that surprised even herself. She poked Cass on the shoulder and continued. "As these people are my witnesses, you will no longer get a free ride here. You will earn your keep just like everyone else. I know you are able to do the tasks you are trained for. I also know you are not as creative as I am. You and I both know you stole several of my ideas last year. That will not be happening again. We have a contract that you will uphold with your own efforts, or I will know why not. I will be watching you. Do I make myself clear?"

"Yes, Mam!" Cass said indignantly. "If there's nothing further, may I be excused?"

"I just wanted to be sure we're both on the same page; that's all. Thank you for the great party," Josie added, falling back on her good manners. "Have a great weekend."

Cass spun around and marched to her office for her purse and left without saying another word. She was obviously fuming over the way Josie had dressed her down in front of the other two.

"Do you think I went too far?" Josie asked Sid and Grams after the door had slammed shut behind Cass. "Do you think she will try something tonight?"

"Nah," Sid said after a pregnant pause. He stood up to put a protecting arm around Josie's shoulders. "Cass is too smart for that. She probably has it figured out the sheriff's department will be patrolling your street, watching your house. Besides, you have all that new surveillance equipment installed there as well as here. You're safe, at least until Monday. Heck, she may even cool down over the weekend. She knows which side of her bread is buttered. With that hefty raise you gave her and no place to go, she won't be leaving in any big hurry."

Just then a tall young man ducked in the door. His blonde hair was windblown. Josie looked at him intently.

His blue jeans and red pocket T-shirt told her he wasn't there for cake and punch.

"Hi, Sid! Hi, ladies!" He greeted. His sky blue eyes lit up with his ready smile.

"Oh, Josie, Eleanor, allow me to introduce Andy Hoverstien," Sid said. "Andy, this is Josie Buchannon, the new owner of Sanderson & Sons. And, this is her grandmother, Mrs. Buchannon. Andy is the new night watchman we talked about, Josie. I told Cass he was the night janitor. Andy, here are the keys to the place. You'll find everything you need in the basement. Remember to take out the trash before you leave in the morning."

"I will, Sid. And, clean the bathroom twice a week, and, yeah, I have the list right here in my pocket," Andy said, patting his shirt pocket and accepting the keys at the same time. "It is very nice to meet you ladies. I hope you had a great party today. Well, I'd better get to work. Don't worry, Miss Buchannon. I'll take care of you and your place." With that, the young man swaggered off in the direction of the basement stairs.

"Time to close up, Josie," Sid said. "get your key out and lock up behind us."

While the weekend was uneventful, Josie couldn't help thinking the other shoe was about to drop. She waited anxiously for her first day on the job as *The Boss*.

The only thing that kept Josie sane was remembering how P.J. had said goodbye to her. As his family had taken turns hugging Josie and congratulating her, P.J. had stood by gazing at her with warmth beaming from his face. When it was finally his turn to greet her, his face had turned pink and he had found a spot on the floor to admire.

"Thank you for coming, P.J.," Josie had broken the silence. "I know it wasn't easy for you to get even one day off. By the way, thank you for the flowers you sent along with the commercial video. They were lovely."

"I wouldn't have missed this day for the world, Josie," P.J. had said. He had looked up then, into her clear blue eyes. "You're welcome for the flowers. I wanted to send more, but Mom said these were already 'ostentatious'."

He had rolled his eyes. His mom could come up with some doozy words as far as he was concerned.

"Listen, Josie. Do you remember that Country Jam Fest that was scheduled for June? The one with Reba on the line-up? Well, it was rained out. They rescheduled it for the last weekend in July. Do you think you'd have time to go with me?" P.J. had asked.

"Well, I guess I'd have to check my datebook and my work schedule," Josie had said, keeping him in suspense. "Actually, now that I'm the boss I can take off whenever I want to. Of course, I'll go with you."

P.J. had been so pleased; he held her shoulders and gave her a quick peck on the lips. Next, he had given her a broad grin.

"Great! I'll call you next weekend to make plans!" With that he had shot out the door and practically leapt into his family's van.

When Monday finally rolled around, Josie felt strung out and needed a little cover-up for the dark circles under her eyes. She managed to make it to the office without any traffic accidents or runs in her nylons. Walking through the front door was easy enough, now that Victoria was the receptionist.

"Good morning, Vikki!" Josie greeted her.

"Good morning, to you, too, Boss!" Vikki replied. She stood up from her desk to hand Josie a pile of envelopes and messages. As she did so, Josie noticed the conservative powder blue dress Vikki was wearing. It was the perfect attire in which to greet clients. "These came for you while you were out. I notated everything and date-stamped your mail. If you have any questions, just buzz me, okay? Have a great day!"

"Thanks!" Josie said and started to walk away. She stopped and turned back to Vikki. "Do you have plans for lunch, today, or could we eat together?"

"I thought you'd never ask!" Vikki said in reply. "We have SO much catching up to do, girl! I have lunch from 12:30 to 1:30 today. Donna goes to lunch early and comes back to man the store while I eat. Will that work for you?"

"It's a date," Josie said, and continued on her way.

Josie greeted every employee on her way through to the last office in the complex. Each one had their own way of acknowledging her. Most of them simply said, "Good morning!" in return. Hildy just grunted and continued working. Josie wasn't offended as she remembered that was just the way Hildy was.

"How's Yanni?" Josie asked her hoping for more than just a guttural response. She was rewarded with an unusual smile from the production worker.

"You remember my cat's name?" Hildy asked. She chuckled. "Yanni's just fine. He's shedding hair all over, as usual; and, he's as fat and sassy as ever."

"That's good. Have a good day, Hildy," Josie said and continued down the hall.

As she approached Cass' office, though, her feet became lead weights and her heart began to palpitate. There was no way around it: in order to perpetuate the charade, she would have to say good morning to her, too. She tentatively edged her head around the door frame and peered inside. Cass was on the telephone with a client, so Josie just smiled and waved. Cass waved half-heartedly and turned away, so Josie slipped into her own office.

Not long afterward, Josie received a call herself. It was an FBI agent requesting the honor of her presence at the café across the street.

"Bring your notebook and pen, make it look like we're working on a business deal," Agent Conrad Malone told her. Collecting the necessary tools, Josie retraced her steps to the front door.

"Vikki, I'm going across the street to the café to meet a client," she informed the receptionist. "I'm not sure how long it will take. Call my cell number if you need me."

Agent Malone had told her he would be wearing a tan blazer and navy pants with a bolo tie. That seemed to be the opposite color combination than most businessmen wear, so Josie figured he would stand out, at least to her. He did; and, she slid into the booth opposite him. Josie also noticed Malone had slick black hair and a Gomez Adams mustache.

"Miss Buchannon. Thank you for being so punctual," the agent greeted her. "Just call me Mr. Malone."

"How do you do?" Josie asked politely and reached out her hand to shake his. "I understand you have a project for me."

"Indeed, I do," Malone said. He laced his fingers and placed them on the table top in front of himself. "I'm willing to reward you handsomely if you can take this on immediately."

"I imagine it will require some late nights at the office, but I think I can manage," Josie continued the coded line of conversation. She opened her notepad and primed her pen. "How can I be of service to you?"

Malone paused long enough to take a casual look around the eating establishment. Josie could tell he had

had plenty of training and experience in covert activities. He was scouting the place for eavesdroppers, she was sure; but, just as certain no one else was aware of it.

"If you could work late every night this week to see what you can draw out of the woodwork, I would really appreciate it. I'm sure you will turn up something of interest to my firm," Malone encoded. He nonchalantly took Josie's pen and wrote something on her pad. She drew it back to the protective custody of her own hands. Glancing down, she read, *You are bait.*

Chapter 17
Staff Meeting

Josie doodled over the heart stopping words to hide them.

"Understood," she said simply. "What happens if I need your … input on anything?"

"I've taken a room upstairs," Malone said with a tilt of his head, indicating directly above them. "I'll be keeping an eye on you."

"That's reassuring," Josie said. "I wouldn't want to make any career-stopping mistakes."

"I understand you have Andy Hoverstien working for you. He's a good kid. Hard worker," the agent said, seeming to change the subject. "He knows his stuff. You can count on him. I'll be in touch."

With that, he slid out of the booth and went to pay for their coffee.

That evening, Josie stayed until 6:30 p.m., went home for a quick bite of supper and returned by 7:15 p.m. She got caught up on her mail and return letters and started on her story boards for the week. It was 10:30 p.m. when she locked up. The place was as silent as a tomb.

Tuesday, everyone was in-house, so she made a point of telling everyone about her new project for Malone and Sons Masonry and that she would be working nights on it. Most of them sympathized with her, but no one volunteered to stay and help.

That evening, just as Josie was about to pack it in, she heard a noise. It sounded like someone had bumped into a chair. Josie took a sharp breath. her heart began to race. Was this it? Was Cass coming to get her already? She quickly flicked a couple of buttons on her computer, the way Andy had shown her, to pull up the security link. A grid of pictures filled the screen, displaying the entire layout of the office. Josie's eyes were quickly glued to grid B-4 where activity could be spotted. She couldn't make out just what or who was there in the dark since the shot was too tiny. Poking at a few more keys, she enlarged the section.

What Josie saw there nearly forced an explosion of laughter out of her. Right there in front of her very eyes was a love fest being acted out on top of Donna Schmidd's desk. Donna and her boyfriend du jour had apparently bumped into the chair as they embraced, slid it aside along with the computer and were necking on the desktop. Josie watched a little longer as Donna pushed her lover away far enough to pull off her blouse and shake out her hair. Today, it had been lime green, Josie remembered. And, Schmidd had worn Gothic black lipstick. The boyfriend sported a leather biker jacket, spiked hair and his own earring. Josie couldn't tell from the angle, but she wouldn't wager a bet against him having his own nose ring, as well. His face was buried in Donna's cleavage, so she couldn't be sure.

All of a sudden, it dawned on Josie that she should put a stop to this. It wasn't professional. Besides, what must Andy be thinking? Surely, he was witnessing the same scene from his basement hide-away. Josie turned to her telephone set and dialed Schmidd's page number.

"Okay, you two, break it up! This is a place of business, not a brothel," Josie intoned. When she looked back at the screen, Donna was frantically scrambling for her blouse and the boyfriend was jerking his head in circles trying to figure out where the voice came from.

"C'mon, Snake! Let's go to my place," Schmidd said and led him toward the door. Josie wasn't far behind them as they left the work site.

Wednesday, Josie received another call from Malone. He told her to turn up the heat. Just how she should to do that, he left up to her. Josie put on her thinking cap and doodled her way onto a second sheet of paper before she had an idea. She called an impromptu staff meeting.

"So, where is everybody at for the week?" Josie asked once everyone was assembled around the conference table. She, of course, was seated at its head with Cass at the foot, glaring at her. "Vikki, what's the status on the mailing project I gave you Monday?"

"All 500 letters are addressed, stamped and ready to run to the post office," Vikki said cheerfully.

"Great! Hildy, what luck have you had with the new animation theory I suggested yesterday?" Josie continued.

Not much for words, Hildy just gave her the thumbs-up sign.

Josie turned toward Cass. She could tell Cass wasn't prepared for this meeting. The displaced dictator had a blank pad in front of her.

"And, Cass, have you come up with any new leads this week?" Josie asked politely. She watched Cass' eyes dart back and forth as she tried to come up with a positive answer. Finally, she gave up. She hiked up the front of her halter dress and sat ramrod stiff. Coven held her head up high and stared Josie straight in the eye.

"I haven't gotten around to that, yet," Cass finally confessed. After a brief pause, she added, "I was too busy doing Internet research for the client I have a meeting with today."

Josie had checked Coven's E-mail history while the employee had been out to lunch yesterday. There were only two items on there for the week; they were the Horoscope and Job Search. Josie made a note to take to Andy about putting a block on Cass' computer so she would be unable to access the Internet and various vital agency documents that were on the share drive. If today's meeting wasn't enough to set Cass off, maybe the "Access Denied" pop-up on her computer would do the trick.

"Perhaps, you should put in an extra hour a day to develop that list," Josie suggested sweetly. "After all, the future of our company depends on generating new leads on a regular basis. Did you bring your campaign ideas for me to preview?"

The answer to that was obvious to everyone in the room. Cass sat nearly empty-handed, with no notes, no story boards, nothing.

"Ah, sorry," Josie feigned an apology. "I can see you didn't. We'll have to catch up later. Mr. Danielson, may we have your report?

The accountant had come prepared. He passed around handouts of the latest profit and loss statement and stood up to display a graph that depicted a flat line in business over the first half the year. Since July 1, the line had soared at a 45 degree angle. His prediction was that it would continue to climb for the remainder of the year and level off after the holidays. A hush fell over the room when he finished. He sat down and looked expectantly at Josie, as did the rest of the prepared staff. Cass sat doodling on her notebook, not daring to look up. Her face was a pasty as the cream color of her baring dress.

Well, Josie thought to herself, *the picture wasn't pretty, but at least no one can accuse Cass of embezzlement ... just murder*. She had to focus on that. She had to continue to push Cass into tipping her hand.

Chapter 18
Baiting the Trap

"Well, I'm glad I came back, then," Josie said, a knot developing in her stomach as she drove the screw in deeper. "Thank you all for your informative reports. Keep up the good work. Meeting adjourned!"

Josie paced herself as she headed back to her office. She wanted to get out of there as fast as she could. She felt an overwhelming desire to run, but she knew she didn't dare. She didn't want to look weak or frightened. She didn't want Cass to know she knew. Josie picked up her briefcase and sped to the door as fast as she could walk.

"I'm going to lunch!" Josie practically shouted at Vikki. "Don't expect me back for a couple of hours. I have my cell phone on for emergencies only."

Josie was long gone before her assistant could answer. She flung herself into her brand new cherry red Bonneville SE, hit the ignition and slammed it into gear. She fled down the highway like a streaking comet. If she had lit the fuse that blew Cass into the next state, she didn't want to hear the explosion. She would take her lumps that night, as the FBI intended. Neither of them figured Cass for a spotlight murderer. It would happen after dark, when no one else was around. In the meantime, Josie didn't want anything to do with a shouting match confrontation.

After she took a dozen or so deep breaths and calmed herself down, Josie fished her cell phone out of her briefcase and punched up Sid's direct line.

"Well, I did it," Josie said breathlessly as Sid answered. "I pushed a few of Cass' buttons. She should be hopping mad at me right about now. I called her bluff by asking for work I knew she didn't have done – and I did it in front of the whole staff. Can you give me Andy's direct number, or can you ask him to do a favor for me?"

"Anything, Josie," Sid said. He always had a calm voice. Nothing seemed to ruffle his feathers – except Lew's murder. "What is it you need? I'll relay the message to him."

"Just in case the show I put on today didn't do the trick, I have another idea," she told Sid as she pulled off the freeway at the little truck stop where she could get something to eat. "Cass has been spending a lot of time on the Internet, searching for a job instead of client research. I checked her E-mail history for the week; and, besides the daily horoscope, that's all that was listed. Granted, she may have found a way to cover up other things; but, she wouldn't delete evidence of honest work. What I want Andy to do is put an Internet block on her computer. If he can zone out those two items, separately, great; if not, block the whole darn thing. I also want to make sure you put the block on our file share so she can't get at any sensitive company data. You did that right in the beginning, didn't you?"

"Yes, yes, of course, I did, Josie. Rest assured; she hasn't gotten access to a speck of important information. Even Danielson locks up his computer at night. Don't worry about that, either. I have his password for you. And, he's got instructions not to give it to anyone but you. No exceptions," Sid said. He kept saying soothing things to Josie until she had had enough. "Okay, then. I'll give Andy a call with his new programming instructions. I think you're right. Cass would be that much more frustrated not being able to use the office Internet. It would seem like the straw that broke the camel's back to her."

With that settled, Josie went inside with her briefcase and ordered chicken fried chicken and waffle fries. She was too distraught to mind her diet. She didn't return to the office until after she had met with her 2 p.m. appointment. Vikki didn't ask any questions; so, Josie didn't have to tell her any lies. The afternoon was filled with returning phone calls and failed attempts at completing several story boards.

Five o'clock rolled around and the office emptied out, each worker bidding Josie good night. With no appetite left after having consumed an entire day's allotment of calories at lunch, Josie called her grandmother and told her she wasn't hungry tonight and wouldn't be home until late.

Then, she flipped on her computer and played a game of Hearts while the Internet connection was made. Selecting a search engine, Josie researched product information on a prospective client and downloaded it. Then, she pressed the right buttons to bring up the security grid. She would feel safer working in a creative funk if she didn't have to try to remember the sequence should a strange noise jar her from her thoughts.

Evening passed swiftly as Josie completed one ad after another. The once-snow-blinding boxes were now filled with colorful renditions of soft-sell activity designed to convince the observer that this product or that service was the one they had been searching for all their lives. Josie looked up from the last box and discovered the sun had gone down. It was pitch black outside the sliding French doors across the hall from her new office. Glancing at the round, magenta clock on the wall near her door, Josie noticed it said 11 p.m. Grams would be worried. She had better get home. It took her all of 40 seconds to sweep the work off her desk and lock all the doors. Cass must have gone to bed already.

Thursday, Cass' computer seemed to have locked her out of the Internet. She came crashing into Josie's office spouting off about the cheap piece of junk she had setting on her desk. Josie nearly asked her to leave because she didn't care to have her ears burning with the four-letter cursings Cass was spewing.

"Sit down and cool off," Josie ordered. She got up, herself, and shut the door. "Cass, would you just chill out. I don't need to be subjected to that kind of language; not here in my own office, not here in this entire office building. I don't care if your computer blew up in your face, you don't have to talk to me in that tone of voice or use those foul four-letter words. This I not a bar; and, I am not your bartender. If you have a legitimate complaint, I will gladly listen. You know my door is always open to my staff. Is that clear?"

Cass fell silent immediately upon hearing her own words reflected back at her. She realized that swearing was unprofessional; so, she glared at Josie instead. She was getting really tired of hearing Josie parrot her own speeches from the not-too distant past.

If this woman was supposed to be so creative, why the hell can't she come up with her own lectures, Cass seemed to be thinking. *Maybe I should just put an end to all this and take her out. I'll have to put my thinking cap on tonight and see what I can come up with.*

"Here's the number for the computer repairman," Josie was saying, she sat there extending a Sticky Note in Cass' direction. "You call him and see when he can come over to have a look at it."

Cass snatched the paper out of Josie's hand and stormed out of her office.

Will tonight be the night? Josie wondered as she watched her go.

Chapter 19
Springing the Trap

Josie spent another long, productive evening at the office the next night. After a while, Josie's mind began to wander. Maybe Cass wasn't the killer. Maybe Lew overdosed himself. Maybe the real killer was long gone. Maybe she was staying late at work for nothing.

Maybe it was time to go home. Josie wasn't thinking straight anymore. All these late nights were getting to her. Josie wrote a note telling Vikki she would be in late tomorrow. She almost added the fib that she had an 8 a.m. interview with a prospective client; but, it wasn't in her to lie. Since she wasn't about to let anyone – except Grams know she was sleeping in – she didn't write a reason.

Lights out. Lock the door. Josie drove home mechanically and crawled into bed without even washing the makeup off her face.

Thunder and lightening woke Josie the next morning. She lay awake listening to it, thinking about the day ahead. This would be the last working day of the week. Cass might even go out of town on the weekend, just to get away from it all, Josie realized. Was there anything left she could use to yank Cass' chain? What more could she do to throw down the gauntlet?

Besides, if I were a murderer, Josie thought, *wouldn't I pick a weekend to 'off' somebody? Having a hotel room in New York City would give me the perfect alibi.*

Wasn't that what Cass' alibi had been the night Lew died? New York City is just an hour – or less – you're back in your room with witnesses to spare.

Hmmm, Josie was getting an idea.

At the office, Josie sat at her desk debating whether or not she should put her new plan into action. She had worn a pantsuit that day, in case the confrontation turned physical. She reached her navy clad arm toward the intercom, and then pulled it back. She reached again, and again snatched back her hand.

Taking a deep breath, she thought to herself, this is it and punched the button. After allowing it to beep on the other end, Josie requested Cass' presence in her office right away. Then she steeled herself for what was about to come. She would have said a prayer, too, if there had been time.

All too soon, Cass was standing in her doorway, clad in her bibbed overalls, white T-shirt and Doc Martin sandals.

"Come in and shut the door, please," Josie instructed Cass. "Have a seat."

"What's up?" Cass asked, almost innocently, as she acquiesced. She crossed her arms in a closed body language that Josie read all too easily.

"The jig's up, that's what's up," Josie said. She watched Cass' expression to gauge how much it would change as she dropped the bomb. "I've figured out what happened to Lew."

At first, Cass' eyes expanded to saucer size as she absorbed Josie's meaning. Just as quickly, though, they narrowed to cat's-eye slits as she realized Josie might be bluffing.

"What do you mean? What happened to Lew? Cass asked suspiciously. "What 'jig'? What are you talking about?"

Cass was exhibiting the same ramrod stiff posture she had in the conference room on Wednesday. She may be a good lier in some cases, but this haute attitude she was displaying belied the truth. Josie was on to something.

"They said Lew died of a drug overdose," Cass said defensively. She started wiggling her right ankle in a nervous tick.

Josie placed her elbows on the desktop and her chin on her folded hands. She just stared into Cass' cat-eyes for a moment before she continued. She hoped it would add a certain air of much-needed confidence to her accusation.

"I have it on good authority you and Lew were lovers," Josie revealed. "I figure you found out you weren't going to inherit the lion's share of the estate and you wanted to get even. Or, you really thought you were going to be the one who inherited the agency when he passed on, and decided to help him along. Or, the two of you needed a pick-me-up in the bedroom scene; so, you accidently OD'd him on Viagra. He could've been on a prescription medication that reacted badly with the Viagra; and, you were left holding the bag. The body bag, that is."

Cass seemed to be squirming a little. Her face was a blossom of red. Josie could see Cass' fingernails digging into the flesh of her upper arm; knuckles, white.

"Are you crazy? First, I was in New York City that night. I have hotel receipts and a clerk who will testify I was there," Cass hissed between clenched teeth. "I told all this to the deputy sheriff. Secondly, I don't remember seeing Lew ever take any kind of drug, let alone Viagra. Lew didn't look like the type of man who would need that sort of thing. Third:

if I had been in love with him, why would I have wanted him dead?"

"Good question; but, here's a better one: Were you in love with him? Or, were you just using him to get the power you craved?" Josie laid it all on the line.

"I don't have to sit here and listen to this crap!" Cass spat as she sprang to her feet. "I've got a client to see. I'm leaving."

She stomped out of Josie's office without so much as a by-your-leave. As dark as her mood was, Josie wasn't about to contradict her. She could just imagine losing her head, literally, if she had tried to stop Cass.

Josie was never so glad to see Andy Hoverstien as she was that day. He sauntered into her office at the stroke of 3 p.m. and greeted her with that down-home country smile he seemed to plaster on his face every day.

"I'm so glad you're here!" she exclaimed. "You just stick around. I won't be going home early tonight, either, unless she does something early. She flew out of here like the proverbial bat-out-of hell. I think I pulled the last string."

Josie's words tumbled out of her mouth pell-mell as she tried to explain to the under-cover cop what had just taken place.

"I believe this is it. It's a good thing Cass thinks you get off work at 8 p.m.," Josie commented as she sunk back onto her office chair. "Ill just bet something's going to go down as soon as she thinks you're out of here."

Listening to the thunder as the rain continued into the evening only increased the dreadful feeling of anxiety that had crept over Josie throughout the afternoon. In spite of the early hour, the cumulonimbus clouds blocked the sun with ominous shadows. Josie flicked her computer screen to display the basement hide-away in order to reassure herself Andy was at his assigned station. He waved at the camera when he realized she was watching him. She waved back at her computer screen; although, she new the camera was hidden somewhere near the ceiling. Then, she went back to her story boards. They were the only things keeping her sane at the moment; although, they presented their own type of problem. It was hard to concentrate on work while anticipating an attack.

Closer to 9:30 p.m., it seemed the sun had dropped out of sight, behind buildings and trees. If Josie's work lamp and computer screen hadn't been on, it would have been pitch black in her office. The silence was deafening.

Then she heard it – the faint click that signified a door locking or unlocking. Which door was it? The front or the back? Josie swiveled back to the computer screen. There she was! Cass was headed down the hall toward her office. She was barely noticeable as she was dressed all in black. Josie froze for a split second, then switched her computer screen to another file and pretended to work on the top story board on her desk.

Suddenly, her door flew open and Cass strode purposefully into the room. The door banged on the wall heard enough that it bounced back and caught Cass in the backside. She grabbed it and slammed it shut. Turning back, Cass scowled at Josie.

"Oh, Cass! You startled me!" Josie exclaimed. "Is that a new outfit? I haven't seen you wear that before. Isn't it rather warm for the middle of summer?"

"Cut the chit-chat!" Cass spat at her and pulled a .22 caliber pistol out of her purse. She aimed it, one-handedly, at Josie. "You're going to have a little accident tonight."

"Wha-what are you doing?" Josie asked, real fear shaking her voice. She cringed in her chair trying to figure out what to do next. She had never anticipated Cass carrying a gun. She figured she would have a knife, like before. Or, maybe try to drug her with a poisoned soda pop. But, this! This was so raw, so unsophisticated. So, *deadly.*

Cass rolled her eyes. She snorted.

"As if you didn't know," she said, her voice dripping with fatal sarcasm. She shook her head and then patted the revolver. "My friend, Colt, here, will take care of a pest problem for me. You see, I just can't have you going around telling people I killed Lew. That just won't do. I can't have our clients getting upset and pulling out over a little thing like that. So, I'm just going to eliminate the problem."

"Well, before you do, grant me one last wish," Josie said, stalling for time. She sat very still so as not to cause Cass to panic and fire prematurely. Andy had to have time to get up here. Besides, a confession on tape wouldn't hurt. "Tell me why you threatened me at knife point and why you killed Lew."

Cass glanced around the dimly lit office and seemed satisfied there were no other witnesses. She set her evil green stare on Josie again.

"Okay," she said, agreeing. "I'll tell you. It's not like you're going to tell anyone else. Not after Colt is through with you."

Cass took a few noisy breaths through the pixie nose on her pouting face and began to whine.

"Lew was sticking up for you no matter what I told him you were trying to do. He didn't believe me when I told him you went behind my back with that company promotion video. He gave you that promotion when I wanted to fire you. You had no reason to leave and get out of my hair; so, I had to make it so you would want to leave on your own. That was the only thing scary enough. Well, besides threatening your grandmother. But, I figured if I scared your grandmother that would just make you want to stay to protect her. This other way worked pretty good, too."

Cass was getting antsy. She shifted from one foot to the other and had to support her gun hand with the other.

"Lew was fun for a while. He was getting old; though, not being able to keep up with my, uh, shall we say, 'appetite'," Cass gave a better-than-thou toss of her shining gold hair. "You were right about the Viagra. Lew's heart medication didn't react well with it at all. And, it looked like it was self-inflicted. Especially since I drove a rental car and stayed at a hotel in New York City. If you grease enough palms in the right part of town, they'll tell anybody anything you want them to."

Where was Andy? Why hasn't he shown up to disarm this crazy woman? Josie was scared stiff. Her heart was racing its way into her throat and sweat began to bead on her forehead.

"You are the last shred of evidence," Cass was saying. She took a better aim and was about to squeeze the trigger when the door burst open and slammed her to the side. At the same time, Josie took a dive to the floor and Cass' gun fired. The bullet lodged itself into the wall behind Josie's cherry wood desk. Peeking around the side of her desk, Josie was startled to see it wasn't Andy who was struggling with Cass for possession of the weapon. It was P.J. Colson. The gun discharged again.

Chapter Twenty-Two
Wrapping It Up

The gun discharged a third time. Both the second and third shots embedded in the ceiling.

Just then, Andy rushed in, sopping wet and bleeding from scratches on his arms, waist and knees. He added his strength to the struggle and came away with the pistol. In two shakes, he had emptied the cartridges onto the floor and shoved the pistol into the back of his jeans. Whipping out a set of handcuffs, he neatly braceletted the offending woman.

"Andy! You're bleeding! What happened to you?" Josie asked. She stood up and edged out in front of the desk. "Where were you, what took you so long?"

"This bitch locked me in the cellar," he said, yanking on the cuffs to test them. "I had to break the basement window and crawl out. It wasn't easy. Those windows were doubly sealed to prevent break-ins."

More visitors arrived. Three men in black, with handguns drawn, crowded into the shrinking room.

"Agent Malone!" Josie greeted, at the same time noticing P.J. had backed himself into a corner. "You're a little late, but welcome to the party."

"Are you hurt, Miss Buchannon?" Malone asked, giving her the once over.

"No, I'm just a little shaken," she replied, then looked back at Andy, holding tightly to Cass. "It's all on tape, right? Make sure you read her her rights. I don't want anything keeping her from her date in prison."

Andy began Miranda-izing Cass. Cass just glared at Josie. Malone finally caught sight of P.J. in the corner.

"Who's that guy?" he asked, jerking his head in Colson's direction.

"He is my boyfriend, Paul Colson, Jr.," Josie said, hoping she wasn't speaking prematurely. "He's from New York City; although, he's been out in the field, on-the-job training. I didn't know he was in town."

"Now that we all know everybody," Cass said, "just how is it you threw this little party; and, I didn't know about the guest list? If you think you're sending me up the river, I have a right to know how you think you're going to do it."

Josie looked questioningly at Agent Malone. He nodded the go-ahead.

"You see, Cass, we had a pretty good idea it was you all along. I remembered smelling that skanky cologne you wear the night I was attacked. And, who else would benefit from Lew's death, but you, if there hadn't been an illegitimate child?" Josie taunted, moving to stand two inches from her assailant. "What you didn't know is just how big Lew's estate was.

"You know all those new clients you signed just before I came back? They were all dummy corporations set up by me using the money and Main Street properties Lew left me. I had to keep you busy while we remodeled the office. The walls have eyes and ears now, thanks to the millions we spent on surveillance equipment and the community service projects. That's right, Cass. I own half the town. And, you own a one-way ticket to the slammer."

Cass hauled back and spat in Josie's face.

"Gentlemen, please add biological assault to the charges," Josie said as she reached for a tissue.

"Come on, men," Malone said. He gestured toward the door. "Let's get her down to the station and process her. Hoverstien, get the surveillance tape. We'll need that for evidence."

The three larger figures in black encircled the waif-sized assailant and ushered her toward the front door.

"Just remember, that's MY collar!" Andy yelled after them. He turned back toward Josie. P.J. had moved to put his arms around Josie to comfort her. "Are you sure you're all right?"

Josie nodded as she held on to P.J.

"Good. Colson, take her home and make sure she gets lots of rest," Hoverstien ordered. "Josie, I'll stop by your place tomorrow to have you fill out a statement."

With that, he disappeared into the basement to retrieve the damning evidence against Cass.

P.J. helped Josie lock up and drove her to her grandmother's house. They cuddled on the sofa and fell asleep in each other's arms. Eleanor had to shake Josie's arm to wake her in the morning.

"Josie! What on earth are you two doing on the couch?" her grandmother asked. "Why didn't you go up to bed? I even made up the guest room for P.J. after he stopped by earlier. It worried me to see that neither bed had been slept in."

"Grams, after the night we had, we just couldn't drag ourselves up the stairs," Josie answered, rubbing her eyes. Then she rolled her head and looked directly into the most beautiful blue eyes she had ever seen. She knew then she was exactly where she wanted to be.

"Come into the kitchen and get your breakfast, you two!" Eleanor ordered and led the way. "You can tell me all about it over a hot cup of tea."

<*>

A month later, Josie found herself in front row seats at the Country Jam Fest being held upstate from Lake City. It was staged in a bowl-shaped depression in some farm meadow. Country Music fans from the tri-state area came out to camp and enjoy the entertainment provided by a dozen different Nashville stars.

"I am a survivor," Ms. Reba McIntyre belted out her encore number, as if by request.

"Hey, P.J.! This is my song!" Josie squealed. She hugged her escort. They both wore blue jeans, western shirts and cowboy boots. It was a far cry from big city office attire; but, they were very fashionable here.

"Our song," P.J. corrected her and hugged her back. Then he reached in his pocket and pulled out a purple plastic Easter egg. He held it up for Josie to see. Her eyes grew wide; and, her breath became short little pants. "This is for you. I haven't stopped thinking about you since the night we met."

They both chuckled as they remembered the mix -up during the middle of the night in the loft above the Colsons' garage. He continued, "My family loves you; and, I love you. Will you marry us? Uh, I mean me. Will you marry me?"

He handed her the purple egg. She pulled the ends apart, gently so as not to drop its precious contents.

"I know it's not Easter; and, this isn't as big as the diamond in the agency ad," P.J. said as he slipped the sparkly ring on her finger, "but, it means so much more to me than acting with Ami."

"Yes! Oh, yes, P.J.! I will marry you!" Josie answered enthusiastically. They embraced. P.J. took Josie's face in his hands and gazed lovingly into her eyes. Then he kissed her long and hard.

"Oh, I almost forgot!" P.J. said as they came up for air. "That interview I had with Lake City Technologies last week came through. They want me to start Monday!"